BROTHER,
CAN YOU SPARE A DIME?

BROTHER,
CAN YOU SPARE A DIME?

THE GREAT DEPRESSION
★ 1929-1933 ★

Milton Meltzer

Illustrated with contemporary prints & photographs

A VINTAGE SUNDIAL BOOK

RANDOM HOUSE   NEW YORK

Vintage Sundial Books are published by Alfred A. Knopf, Inc., Pantheon Books, and Random House, Inc.

First Vintage Sundial Edition, January 1973. Originally published by Alfred A. Knopf, Inc., in the Living History Library in 1969.

Library of Congress Cataloging in Publication Data
Meltzer, Milton, 1915-   Brother, can you spare a dime? The great depression, 1929-1933.
(A Vintage sundial book, VS-6)   Original ed. issued in series: The Living history library. Bibliography. p.   1. United States—Economic conditions—1918-1945.   2. United States—Social conditions—1918-1932.   3. Depressions—1929—United States.   I. Title. (thru dime)   [HC106.3.M37 1973]   309.1′73′0916   72-2910
ISBN 0-394-70806-7

CONTENTS

BROTHER,
CAN YOU SPARE A DIME?

A DIFFERENT DEPRESSION

Half the people in America today are too young to remember the Great Depression of the 1930s. Their parents
remember, and certainly their grandparents. Whether
they were rich or poor, bankers or laborers, they remember.

Probably they never talk about it. People like to talk
about the "good old days." They don't like to recall the
bad days. Not when the days became weeks and months
and years, and years, and years. Years that made wounds
that never healed.

It was the stock-market crash of October 1929 that
signaled the slide into the pit. At first it seemed to be only
another depression—they would not start calling it the
Great Depression for some time. After all, America had
already gone through seventeen or more depressions.
Could another one be any worse?

Every generation before 1929 had experienced a time of
mass unemployment. Often it happened several times in
one man's life span. A chart of the nation's economic
cycle shows that downturns generally occurred every five
to ten years. Some lasted longer than others and brought
greater hardships. Usually the slide into the pit was steep,

and the climb out of the depths slow.

But the depression that began in 1929 was different. It came on harder and faster, it engulfed a larger part of the population, it lasted much longer, and it did far more and far worse damage than any before it.

No one can understand the America of today without knowing something about the Great Depression of the 1930s. Many of the millions who suffered through it are still alive. Theirs and their children's and their grandchildren's lives are different because of that disaster. The government we live under, the laws that regulate us, the traditions we hold to—all were reshaped by the pressures of those terrible years.

How it started, and why, and what it felt like to be sucked down into the whirlpool will be told in these pages.

The book begins in the 1920s and ends in the spring of 1933. The depression did not stop that year. It lasted through the Thirties, and it is said on good evidence that for some it *never* ended. But this book is not a chronology or an economic study of those hard times. Rather, it is the story of the human side of the Great Depression: what happened to auto workers and wheat farmers, to sales clerks and secretaries, to teachers and doctors, to miners and sharecroppers, to old folks and children, to white and to black. It relates the impressions those first few and worst years made on many Americans, including the author, who lived through them.

First let us look at America on the eve of the crash. How well off was the nation in those gay and prosperous Twenties?

★ 2 ★

A DOLLAR FOREVER

"We have not yet reached the goal, but given a chance to go forward with the policies of the last eight years, and we shall soon, with the help of God, be within sight of the day when poverty will be banished from the nation." So said Herbert Hoover on August 12, 1928, in his speech accepting the Republican nomination for President.

Hoover spoke for most middle-class people. They thought the American dream of unlimited plenty was close to fulfillment. The huge industrial machine that had begun building up during the Civil War had reached fantastic heights of mass production. Assembly lines poured out products by the millions, while advertising stimulated the consumer to buy them. From privy, icebox, and buggy the country moved almost overnight into the New Era of bathrooms, electric refrigerators, and automobiles. Washing machines, vacuum cleaners, and telephones promised to make life easier and more convenient. Homemade amusements gave way to radio and the movies. American business and American salesmanship had put the nation aboard an express train rushing toward permanent prosperity.

The Twenties opened with the election to the presidency of a small-town, poker-playing newspaper publisher, Warren G. Harding. The Ohio Republican piloted the country's return to what he called "normalcy" after World War I. Woodrow Wilson's crusade to "make the world safe for democracy" was over; now it was time to relax.

The good-time years began with government scandals over the exploitation of public lands by private oil interests. A Senate exposure sent one Cabinet member to jail, and others among Harding's White House cronies committed suicide or fled the country.

Harding died in office in 1923, and a prim, purse-mouthed Yankee, Calvin Coolidge, stepped up from the vice-presidency. Under the campaign slogan of "Keep Cool with Coolidge" he won the 1924 election for the Republicans. "The business of America is business," he announced, and doing little and saying less, he soon built a reputation for wisdom. As he saw it, his job was to "prevent crime and preserve contracts." Soon irrepressible wits were circulating a thousand jokes about him: "Did you hear? President Coolidge is dead!" "How can they tell?"

While the old-fashioned, frugal Vermonter lived quietly in the White House, in the nation thrills and novelties, trifles and fads, sports and games appealed to millions tired of political and social problems. The era was soon tagged the Roaring Twenties. The Eighteenth Amendment—prohibiting the making, sale, or transportation of alcoholic liquors—had gone into effect in 1920, and those who did not bother with home-brewing happily did business with rumrunners and bootleggers. Cynicism over lawbreaking lifted gangsters like Al Capone to great power and wealth. That they moved in respectable social circles showed how much success was approved, no matter how obtained. It began to seem hopelessly old-fashioned to have moral scruples. Other celebrities of the Twenties were the kings of sport—Jack Dempsey, Helen Wills, Red Grange, Bobby Jones.

When the newspapers were not heralding heroes such as Lindbergh, who flew the Atlantic, or Babe Ruth, who hit sixty homers in one season, they were front-paging the sex scandals of millionaires and movie stars. Publicity and advertising ballyhooed everything from an imported Chinese game, mah-jongg, to bathing beauty contests at Atlantic City, to real estate in Florida, where swampy lots sometimes changed hands ten times in one day, selling at prices incredibly above their real value.

The stock market was soaring and prosperity was in full flood in 1928 when Calvin Coolidge chose not to run again. Instead, his Secretary of Commerce, Herbert Hoover, was nominated by the Republicans. A hardworking engineer of major accomplishments, Hoover ran against Alfred E. Smith, then Governor of New York. An Irish Catholic, Smith represented an increasingly urban America; he also made abolishing prohibition his chief campaign issue. Smith was the more liberal candidate, though both parties appealed openly to big business. But good times always favor the party in power, and many voters objected to Smith because of his religion. Hoover won the election with a majority of 58 percent of the popular vote. Gloom in the Democratic ranks was so thick that some predicted the party was on its deathbed.

Herbert Hoover took office in March 1929, confident in his own campaign prediction that the policies he had

helped shape over the preceding eight years would soon banish poverty from the nation.

In the *New York Times* of May 7, 1929, a full-page advertisement placed by *True Story* magazine trumpeted:

You business executives sitting at your desks, you have been making a fairy tale come true. Within ten years you have done more toward the sum total of human happiness than has ever been done before in all the centuries of historical time.

Behind the business executives was technology. Specialized machines were at work in almost every aspect of production. In the factories between 1919 and 1929 horsepower per wage earner went up 50 percent and output per man-hour rose 72 percent. By 1929 workers could make each unit in 30 percent less time. The national income rose from $61 billion in 1922 to $87 billion in 1929, or almost 44 percent.

Yes, the Twenties were a very good time for many Americans. More were doing well and living comfortably than ever before. Business profits spiraled rapidly upward, over 80 percent in that decade, climbing much higher than productivity. It was a time to get rich quickly, and it looked like it could be done without much effort. A speculative fever took hold. Even the collapse of the Florida land boom in mid-decade did not cool it off. Those who gave up gambling on the Florida climate believed they could get rich just as effortlessly by gambling on the stock market. Why not, when the papers reported in 1926 that the Mellon family had made $300 million just on aluminum and oil stocks? By that time the ticker

The Lindbergh parade down Broadway in 1927.

tape seemed to have become the heart of the economy, endlessly pumping out stock-market quotations. In 1929 a million and a half people were trading in the market. And, trying to get rich quick, many of them bought stock on margin, paying only part of the purchase price. Those making big profits shoveled them back into the market, driving stock prices higher and higher. How could you lose?

Of course, there were working people who had no extra funds to play with. In 1929 the Brookings Institution, an economic research group, made a national study of family income. Of the country's 27.5 million families, 21.5 million, or 78 percent, were not doing so well. They earned under $3,000 a year. Among them were 6 million families with incomes under $1,000 a year.

The 21.5 million families earning under $3,000, the study reported, were able to save nothing at all. Yet appeals to buy were dinned in their ears hour after hour on radio, and the movies teased them with fantasies of beautiful people living frivolous lives in luxurious surroundings. No matter how alluring the advertisements of new products, how could they buy?

Salesmen had an answer: offer the goods on credit. Soon almost anything could be bought on the installment plan. By 1929 three out of every four cars were being financed on time. The cautious American habit of buying only what you could pay for in cash gave way to a philosophy of "a dollar down and a dollar forever." You took a chance on buying now because you believed business would keep prospering, and you, too, would have more money. So why not buy that Model T today, while you were young?

A scene from the 1928 movie called "Mad Hour,"
with Alice White and Sally O'Neil. The bootleg
liquor in the flask was undoubtedly diluted.

Gambling on the stock market was another way of gambling on the future. Speculation was so widespread that the number of stockbrokers jumped from 30,000 in 1920 to 71,000 by the end of the decade. Few working people bought stocks or even thought of doing so, but still, brokers urged them into the market. "I am firm in my belief," said John J. Raskob, a General Motors magnate and Al Smith's campaign manager, "that anyone not only can be rich, but ought to be rich." If a man saved only $15 a week, Raskob advised, and put it into good stocks, in 20 years he would have at least $80,000 and an income from investments of $400 a month. He would be rich!

But how many Americans even in those flush times could save fifteen dollars a week? The Brookings study reported that three out of four families were able to save nothing.

The gap between incomes was wide. The 27,500 wealthiest families in America had as much money as the 12 million poorest families. The nation's top and bottom were worlds apart. While miners and lumbermen earned about $10 a week, Andrew Mellon was paying an income *tax* of $1,883,000, Henry Ford a tax of $2,609,000, and John D. Rockefeller, Jr., a tax of $6,278,000.

During the Twenties, Mellon was Secretary of the Treasury in the Cabinets of Presidents Harding, Coolidge, and Hoover. His goal was to cut government spending and reduce taxes. By 1928, as the wave of prosperity carried large capital investors to new peaks of income, he succeeded in drastically chopping the income tax of the very rich. During that decade the income of the rich from dividends, interest, and rent rose by almost 30 percent. By 1929 the 5 percent of Americans with the highest income were taking in about one third of all personal income.

How much unemployment was there during the prosperous Twenties?

There can be no hard answer, because before the mid-1930s the country showed little interest in such problems. Government agencies did not gather adequate data. One clue, however, lies in the Bureau of Labor Statistics records between 1924 and 1929. In those five years the number of industrial workers listed as temporarily laid off averaged 14 percent. In the worst month, July 1924, it was as high as 25 percent. Even at the peak of the 1929 boom, unemployment amounted to 7 or 8 percent.

Two estimates exist for the number of unemployed in September 1928. Professor Horace Taylor of Columbia University reported that his studies showed that "the number of unemployed in the country at the present time is about 4,000,000." Senator Robert F. Wagner of New York said the figure was nearer 5.8 million.

Whole regions of the country felt the weight of these statistics. The textile towns of New England, the Allegheny coal towns, the Deep South, the shipbuilding and shoe-manufacturing centers of the North suffered hard times all through the 1920s. And farmers everywhere. Prices of farm produce slipped badly after World War I, and never made their way up again.

The majority of Americans lived at or below a bare comfort level. Still, for those who were working life was a little better than it had been. More people were doing well than ever before: in 1929 one half of America's families owned a car. There was a trend upward, however slight. And when a workingman looked abroad and saw how workers in other lands lived, or looked back to the mean life he or his immigrant forebears had fled from, he knew his standard of living was one of the best in the world.

PANIC

Sixteen-year-old Gordon Parks, later to become a leading photographer, was living alone in St. Paul and feeling very contented during the pleasant summer of 1929. The young black had a job as a bellboy at the exclusive Minnesota Club. He had just earned a two dollar raise and then, when September came, he began classes at Central High School, switching to part time on his job.

Working evenings and weekends at the club [he wrote] I overheard talk of Hoover, A.T. & T., General Motors, U.S. Steel, General Electric, the Federal Reserve Bank and other such names. And, although I didn't know what the conversations really meant, I sensed a certain optimism in them . . .

The employees' locker room at the club was unusually quiet when I arrived at work on Wednesday. Waiters who had known each other for years were sitting about as though they were strangers. The cause of the silence was tacked to the bulletin board. It read: "Because of unforeseen circumstances, some personnel will be laid off the first of next month. Those directly affected will be notified in due time. The management."

"That Hoover's ruining the country," an old waiter finally said. No one answered him. I changed into my suit of blue tails, wondering what had happened.

By Thursday the entire world knew. "MARKET CRASHES—PANIC HITS NATION!" one headline blared. The newspapers were full of it, and I read everything I could get my hands on, gathering in the full meaning of such terms as Black Thursday, deflation and depression. I couldn't imagine such financial disaster touching my small world; it surely concerned only the rich. But by the first week of November I too knew differently; along with millions of others across the nation, I was without a job. All that next week I searched for any kind of work that would prevent my leaving school. Again it was, "We're firing, not hiring." "Sorry, sonny, nothing doing here." Finally, on the seventh of November I went to school and cleaned out my locker, knowing it was impossible to stay on. A piercing chill was in the air as I walked back to the rooming house. The hawk had come. I could already feel his wings shadowing me.

On the Wednesday young Parks described—October 23, 1929—there had been an unexpected, severe break in stock-market prices. Several weeks of storm warnings had come first. Wall Street was feeling jittery, and now the anxiety boiled up in speculators all across the country. The next day, Thursday, October 24, prices plunged sickeningly. They fell faster and faster that morning, and by eleven o'clock it was like an avalanche. Panic had seized the market. Wild rumors swept Wall Street. That day almost 13 million shares changed hands.

A *New York Times* reporter described the scene:

Fear struck the big speculators and little ones, big investors and little ones. Thousands of them threw their holdings into the whirling Stock Exchange pit for what they would bring. Losses were tremendous and thousands of prosperous brokerage and bank accounts, sound and healthy a week ago, were completely wrecked in the strange debacle . . . The entire financial district was thrown into hopeless confusion and excitement. Wild-eyed speculators crowded the brokerage offices, awed by the disaster which had overtaken many of them.

The big bankers tried to come to the rescue: they pooled their resources to halt the collapse. Prices moved up a little during the afternoon, but within a few days the avalanche roared down again.

On Monday, October 28, the losses were much worse. The next day, Tuesday, was what historians have called "the most devastating day in the history of markets." Sixteen million shares were sold, and many put up for sale could find no buyers, no matter how low the price. As the spools of ticker tape with their printed numerals unwound, men saw their fortunes and their hopes disappear.

The worst had happened, it was thought. But not yet. The worst grew worse and worse. The panic went on smashing prices. It was mid-November before the market stopped falling—for a time. In those few weeks $30 billion had blown away—the same amount of money America had spent on World War I!

To the great majority of working people and farmers, the stock market was a remote operation they knew little

WORST STOCK CRASH STEMMED BY BANKS;
12,894,650-SHARE DAY SWAMPS MARKET;
LEADERS CONFER, FIND CONDITIONS SOUND

FINANCIERS' EASE TENSION | *Wall Street Optimistic After Stormy Day;*
Clerical Work May Force Holiday Tomorrow | **LOSSES RECOVERED IN PART**

URGE A NEW PARK AV. BUILT ABOVE TRACKS FROM 96TH ST. NORTH

STOCKS GAIN AS MARKET IS STEADIED;
BANKERS PLEDGE CONTINUED SUPPORT;
HOOVER SAYS BUSINESS BASIS IS SOUND

Mayor's Traffic Advisers Ask Decking Over of Viaduct to Both Building Lines.

President Hoover Issues a Statement of Reassurance
On Continued Prosperity of Fundamental Business | **TRADING IS NEAR NORMAL**

EUROPE IS DISTURBED BY AMERICAN ACTION ON OCCUPATION DEBT

STOCK PRICES SLUMP $14,000,000,000
IN NATION-WIDE STAMPEDE TO UNLOAD;
BANKERS TO SUPPORT MARKET TODAY

London Urges an Explanation of Move for Direct Payments by Germany.

Sixteen Leading Issues Down $2,893,520,108;
Tel. & Tel. and Steel Among Heaviest Losers | **PREMIER ISSUES HARD HIT**

STOCKS COLLAPSE IN 16,410,030-SHARE DAY,
BUT RALLY AT CLOSE CHEERS BROKERS;
BANKERS OPTIMISTIC, TO CONTINUE AID

LEADERS SEE FEAR WANING | *240 Issues Lose $15,894,818,894 in Month;*
Slump in Full Exchange List Vastly Larger | **CLOSING RALLY VIGOROUS**

Optimistic headlines from the New York Times
despite the disaster on Wall Street.

about and Wall Street was only an awesome name. But there were a million and a half people trading on the market. Those who had bought on margin now had to beg, borrow, or steal money in the useless attempt to hold their stocks. Overnight the life savings of many went down the drain.

The shock was terrible, but most people could not really believe what was happening. On October 25, the day after the crash, President Hoover had reassured the nation: "The traditional business of the country, that is, production and distribution of commodities, is on a sound and prosperous basis." On November 4, Henry Ford announced: "Things are better today than they were yesterday." On November 15, Hoover spoke to the newspapers again: "Any lack of confidence in the economic future of the basic strength of business in the United States is foolish." And on December 10, the Chairman of the Board of Bethlehem Steel, Charles M. Schwab, declared: "Never before has American business been as firmly entrenched for prosperity as it is today."

The boat was only listing a little; there was no danger of it going down. Optimism would save it.

But the Great Depression had begun.

How did it happen?

The causes have been investigated ever since 1929. No one believes that any single cause can account for the Great Depression. Economists think it was rather a combination of several. There is some debate over which causes were more important, but these at least seem to have been basic:

1. On one hand business had kept prices and profits high. Through the 1920s business had grown bigger and bigger, and the monopolies that developed were able to control prices. They made high profits and put them back into more production, so as to make still more profits. At the same time business kept wages low, and that meant labor didn't get enough to buy its share of what it had produced. If business had distributed its earnings more widely through higher wages, people would have been able to buy more.

2. Farmers had been in a bad way since World War I, when they had produced more than ever before to feed and clothe the armies and peoples of Europe. After the war the farmers kept up their high level of production even though Europe's farmers were back at work again. So surpluses piled up. With supply greater than demand, the farmers had to accept lower prices. Then they had too little income to buy what the factories were turning out.

3. The postwar boom years had encouraged industry to build more and bigger plants. Soon they were able to produce far more than they could sell.

4. Improved technology meant more goods could be produced by fewer workers. Labor-saving machinery began putting men out of jobs in industry after industry. With fewer people employed, less money was paid out in wages and there was less money to buy the goods coming off the production lines.

A few weeks after the crash this H. T. Webster cartoon—
"The Thrill That Comes Once In a Lifetime"
—appeared in the Herald Tribune.

5. Business was shaky throughout the world during the 1920s. The countries of Europe were overloaded with debts and taxes that World War I had brought on.

6. Credit was so easy to obtain that great numbers of people piled up debts as they ventured into new businesses or bought heavily on the installment plan. Using their profits or by borrowing, people turned the stock market into a gambling machine. They were willing to pay high prices for stocks in the hope that they could sell them at even higher prices. Soon stock prices were far beyond the real value of businesses. The balloon expanded and expanded. When it finally burst, stockholders rushed to sell, fearing that stock prices would drop even further. And so they did.

All these weaknesses underlay the operation of a complicated economic system at the time of the crash in 1929. Wages and prices, trade and investment, production and consumption, machinery and manpower were not regulated by government and could be thrown wildly off balance. When the panic struck Wall Street on that October day in 1929, it was like the breach in the levee that releases the devastating floodwaters.

★ | 4 | ★

GIVE ME BACK MY JOB AGAIN

Within two months the crash of the stock market had thrown several million people out of work. The trouble spread quickly. Many businesses came to a dead halt. Salespeople were fired from stores, factories cut down on production, executives decided not to expand. Recently completed office buildings, apartment houses, and hotels could find few tenants. Construction ground to a standstill. Banks tightened up on credit, and business and industry ran dry of funds. And as the wheels slowed down, and then stopped, pink slips began to appear in pay envelopes—the deadly notice that your company no longer needed you.

Some industries and cities were hit sooner than others. In New England's textile towns, layoffs were an old story. The trouble had begun for them in the mid-1920s. A year after the crash three out of seven millhands were not working. The writer Louis Adamic, wandering through what he called the "tragic towns," told of the idle men he saw in Lawrence, Massachusetts:

I saw men standing on the sidewalks clapping their hands in a queer way, obviously just to be doing some-

thing. I saw men talking to themselves, walking around, stopping, looking into shop windows, walking again.

For several minutes I watched an elderly man who stood on a deserted corner near the enormous and idle Everett Mills in the posture of an undotted question mark. He did not see me. Every now and then he swung his arms, not because it was cold, but no doubt because he wanted activity other than walking around, which he probably had been doing for years in a vain effort to get a job. He mumbled to himself. Then, suddenly, he stepped off the curb and picked up a long piece of string from a pile of rubbish, and his big, work-eager hands began to work with it, tying and untying feverishly. He worked with the string for several minutes. Then he looked around and, seeing me, dropped the string, his haggard, hollow face coloring a little, as though from a sense of guilt, or intense embarrassment. He was shaken and confused and stood there for several seconds, looking down at the rubbish heap, then up at me. His hands finally dropped to his sides. Then his arms swung in a sort of idle reflex motion and he turned, hesitated a while as if he did not know where to go and finally shuffled off, flapping his arms. I noticed that his overcoat was split in the back and that his heels were worn off completely.

Nineteen-thirty—it was a year the *New York Times* ushered out with these words: "You cannot help feeling sorry for the stars and nebulae many light years away who still have the year 1930 coming to them."

The auto industry shrank like a punctured balloon. Certainly no one would make a down payment on a

Model T or Stutz Bearcat now. The Willys plant in Toledo dropped from 28,000 workers in March 1929 to 4,000 in November. In Detroit it was no better. The Ford payroll—128,000 in March—sank to 100,000 in December. Eighteen months later it had dwindled to 37,000.

Here is Robert Cruden, an unemployed Detroit auto worker, writing early in 1931 for the *New Republic* magazine:

"Nobody's buyin' autos any more."

This was the remark which greeted us as we joined the 200 men huddled together across the road from the Ford Rouge employment office. We were all former Ford workers—some of us had been laid off in October, 1929; some last summer, and some of us after New Year's when the newspapers were shrieking "Ford Hiring 75,000!" Many of the men had their badges, having never been officially "laid off." They were there with the rest of us, shivering in the cold, hoping against hope that Ford would start hiring . . .

"It ain't no use," a millwright was saying, "I went in to get a pass from my boss an' he said, 'Good God, man, we're layin' off.' "

"Yeah, that's true," added a toolmaker in a hopeless voice. "My cousin says there ain't 25,000 workers left in the whole plant."

"That means about a hundred thousand laid off," murmured another.

More and more men arrived on the line. Many of them displayed their badges, shining in the cold sunlight.

"Ah don' know what ah'm goin' t' do," spoke up a

carpenter. "They done lay me off a year ago Octobah an' ah ain't worked since."

"They'll have to do something pretty damn quick," said a crankshaft worker sullenly . . .

Two and a half miles to Fisher Body. Two hours at Ford Rouge had frozen us out—we were not clad for that biting wind which numbed our feet and chilled our bodies. The Fleetwood plant of Fisher—the biggest body plant in the world—the employment office packed.

"Ever work for Fisher?" a watchman demanded.

"No."

"Then get out!"

Out in the cold again. The wind blew up from the river in icy gusts, chilling us to the marrow through our worn suits and cotton workshirts. Even those of us with overcoats were cold.

"Gawd, my feet's sore," said one. His shoes, of different makes, were cracked and cut; the soles were parting from the uppers.

Not knowing what to do next we stood talking. When would things pick up?

"Maybe in a coupla years," suggested a young machinist.

"Never," ejaculated an old die-maker. "Too many machines. They kin put out all the autos they need with the men they got."

"Things can't pick up till we get back to work," said a tinsmith. "How'd they expect us to buy autos when we can't buy food?"

"Yeah, an' it'll take us another ten years to pay our debts when we do go back to work," said a Chrysler worker with an air of finality.

On the tramp again, our heads bent in the wind, hands stuck deep in pockets, our feet sore and tired.

"I'm glad I ain't married," someone said . . .

Before it was daylight we were on the way to Chevrolet. The darkness seemed to intensify the coldness. In front of the L. A. Young plant a dozen boys were huddled together, the oldest about eighteen. Pale and cold, yet sleepy, they cowered in the wind. Some of them did not have overcoats. They stared at us as we hurried on.

The police were already on the job, waving us away from the Chevrolet employment office. "Nothin' doin'. Nothin' doin'." . . .

Scores of former Chevrolet workers were here—but they were not being hired.

Now we were tramping through falling snow, a cold and hungry line. After a half hour we reached the Hamtramck plant of Briggs Body. It was boarded up . . .

Down on one side of the street we marched, toward the Dodge plant. On the other, a steady line of men and women tramped away from it. My partner told me how he had to pawn his micrometers, costing $16, for $2.50. He had been forced to live with his brother, who had five children and who had himself been laid off just two weeks previously. "We gotta do somethin'," he growled.

Dodge employment office. A big well fed man in a heavy overcoat stood at the door saying "No, no," as we passed before him.

Women everywhere on the road to Murray Body. Native born and foreign born, young women and old women, women with whole fingers and women with hands mangled in the presses—a continuous stream of them passing and repassing, looking for jobs.

"It's come so that the women an' kids have to work now," said a Hudson worker bitterly.

Murray Body wasn't hiring. It was laying off its own workers, to whom it pays fifteen cents an hour.

On the tramp again. A young worker, married and father of two children, burst out, "A worker's got no right to have kids any more."

When the depression hit one-industry towns, such as Detroit or Lowell, the effect was disastrous and very visible. Cities with varied industry suffered severely too, although it was often harder to notice. The Metropolitan Life Insurance Company checked its industrial policy-holders in forty-six of the biggest cities in December 1930 and found that almost 24 percent were unemployed. In 1931, 18 percent of Cincinnati's working people were jobless and 19 percent employed only part time. In Buffalo, the percentages were worse: 26 and 21.

Early in 1931 Louis Stark, a reporter, visited the New York City Free Employment Bureau to see what kind of men were looking for work:

I sweep the scene before me. A thousand men are in the loft. The front line is ten feet away. A stout rope is stretched from pillar to pillar. Behind the rope the men are herded. Men? Many are boys, still in their teens; a few, very few, rosy-cheeked youngsters; the rest old beyond their time. Shoulders broken by responsibility. Faces that look into a black abyss.

The room is almost silent. A slight, despairing hum from the job seekers. Patient, stretched on the rack of a social system that compels this degradation, they stand quite mute. The suspense is painful. Behind the desks near me the clerks sit with pencils poised. Waiting. A telephone bell rings. A new job! A hurried conversation. A card is filled out, handed to the "auctioneer," a gray-haired man, round faced, with curling mustaches. Grasping his megaphone and stepping briskly on a dais, he shouts: "Man wanted to repair typewriter, four hours work, fifty cents an hour. Desk Number 2."

There is a movement in the crowd. The jellied mass quivers. Half a dozen men squirm out. They throw themselves at desk Number 2. Work, blessed blessing, is within their grasp, perhaps. They overwhelm the clerk with a torrent of appeals.

"Please, mister, I'm a good mechanic."

"Please, I gotta family."

"Gimme a chance."

Swiftly the clerk selects two men. The lucky competitors dash from the room with the precious cards in their fists, each hoping to "beat the other fellow to it." Two are sent for each job listed so that the employer may have a choice.

The clerk turns back to his desk. With leaden feet the four disappointed men move slowly back and merge again with the patient mass. A thousand desperate souls—minus two—freeze again into a mute appeal. Until a telephone again rings.

"One sandwich man, a dollar and a half a day. Desk Number 4."

A 1932 drawing by George Grosz, the German artist.
Witness to the mass unemployment of his own country
in the Twenties, he saw it over again here in the Thirties.

OUTSIDE AN EMPLOYMENT AGENCY

This time a dozen fling themselves at the desk. You are struck by their youth. Here is a boy, seventeen, begging for the job. Here a skilled mechanic of thirty. Several laborers, none over forty or so. Again two are selected. They dash off hysterically. In the others, hope, faintly flickering, dies to a low black flame.

Half a dozen times the scene is reënacted. An hour passes. The loft is cleared to make way for another thousand who have been waiting in the cold. The applicants, Director E. C. Rybicki will tell you, are handled in five shifts. Waiting two hours in line outside and one hour inside prevents more than one turn a day.

Five thousand men, on the average, ask for work daily in this loft. On Monday there are more. Once or twice it was ten thousand. Perhaps three or four hundred get jobs. Nearly all are temporary, from an hour to several days.

Whether you were a skilled mechanic or a boy of seventeen, any job at all would do. A new song was heard: "I Don't Want Your Millions, Mister."

I Don't Want Your Millions, Mister

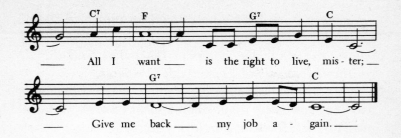

All I want is the right to live, mister; Give me back my job again.

I don't want your Rolls-Royce, mister,
I don't want your pleasure yacht.
All I want is food for my babies;
Give me my old job back.

Think me dumb if you wish, mister,
Call me green, or blue, or red.
This one thing I sure know, mister:
My hungry babies must be fed.

We worked to build this country, mister,
While you enjoyed a life of ease.
You've stolen all that we built, mister;
Now our children starve and freeze.

People grasped at straws to find the answers to questions that were almost too hard to bear. *Harper's Monthly* observed:

Fortune tellers are flourishing as never before in generations. The drawing of horoscopes, numbering of names, staring at glass balls, table-tipping, and muttering over teacups find an increasingly large number of believers. One million three hundred thousand radio listeners in a year respond by mail to Evangeline Adam's tri-weekly broadcasts; a million and a half a year ask the astrologer Dolores for advice; a magazine article about an unnamed sooth-sayer brings 11,700 inquiries; newspapers print daily horo-scopes, the astral predictions of Belle Bart, and the algorithmic forecasts of Elaine Hale Williams. . . .

In all astrological clienteles women used to predomi-nate, but now there is an equal number of men. Women used to ask, How can I hold my husband or get rid of him? Shall I meet the right man? Shall I become engaged this year? . . . Since October, 1929, however, the greatest number of inquiries from both men and women have to do with the earning of daily bread.

For those who sought relief in humor, there was *Ballyhoo* magazine. It printed, for example, this spoof matrimonial ad: "Now at liberty. I am an unemployed ventriloquist, expert at dish wiping and putting out cat. Prefer woman of 30, with money in government bonds, or in safe deposit vault. Will even consider children if they have good jobs."

Some of the jobless could tell their own story of the hunt for work. Karl Monroe, a reporter laid off after nine years' experience in New England, came to New York City in early 1930 to look for a job.

The round of newspaper offices and news bureaus netted me a series of polite but firm statements to the effect that "there's nothing open just now, but you might leave your name and address." After two weeks of this I set myself to what I believed would be the much easier task of secur-ing a clerical place, or even something like ushering in a theater, "hopping the bells" at a hotel, or running an elevator in an office building.

Innocently enough, I followed the crowd to the agencies in Sixth Avenue. Visions of being sent to a position where a percentage would be taken from the first month's salary for a fee were quickly dissolved in the face of the cold fact that any position must be paid for in full and in advance. I learned from one young man that he had paid $10 for a job at which he had worked only four days, receiving $13.50, or a net profit of $3.50 for his four days of work. He and other victims told me, apparently from experience, that many of the agencies make a regular practice of sending men to jobs for which they are obviously unfitted, so that the same job might be sold several times. Many of the men, I learned, realized this, but were willing to "take a gypping" in order to earn a few dollars.

My funds were getting low, and rather than spend any more of the bit of cash I still had I resolved to ride the subways for the night. Not only did I find this fairly easy, but I found that hundreds of others were doing it. Experts at the game—men who live a hand-to-mouth existence by panhandling and petty racketeering—told me that the most satisfactory system was to ride the B.M.T. trains which run from Times Square to Coney Island, swinging around a loop and returning. The trip consumes nearly two hours if a local train is taken. A good corner seat gives the rider a chance to get a fair nap, and the thing can be repeated endlessly. When morning came I went to the Grand Central Terminal, where I washed for a nickel.

Sleeping in the parks, I found, was much less satisfactory than the comfort offered by the rapid transit companies. Tired, hungry, and cold, I stretched out on the bench, and despite the lack of downy mattress and comforter eventually fell asleep. The soles of my feet were swollen with blisters because my shoes had not been removed in at least seventy-two hours and I had tramped the sidewalks for three days. Suddenly I was awakened by a patrolman who had swung his night stick sharply against the soles of my feet, sending an indescribable electric pain through my hunger racked body.

Unemployment in the 1930s meant, first of all, doing without necessities—physical deprivation. But being out of work did terrible damage to the human spirit as well. Helen Hall, a social work pioneer, helped conduct a study for the National Federation of Settlements on the effects of unemployment on people in thirty cities. In the summer of 1930 she reported some examples of what the study disclosed:

We didn't know that one of the fathers in our Philadelphia neighborhood was out of work until we wondered why his small son's legs grew thin. The man was a roofer, and for four months his family of nine had lived on the $7 which fifteen-year-old Joe made as errand boy in a drug store. This had been supplemented by $3.80 for a day's work when Mr. Raymond shoveled snow for the city, and $10 which he had earned by roofing the house of a man in his old firm. "He's always walking or looking," said his wife. "The places are so far apart that his feet get sore. He's been everywhere—the day shifts and the night shifts. We had to put cotton in the heels of his shoes. Sometimes he don't know where he's walking. He's been back so often they hold up their hands when they see him coming."

As the jobless shuffled onto breadlines in the early days of the depression, some observers noticed that they were always men. Where were the women? There must certainly be women in want, yet they were never seen in these lines.

Emily Hahn, reporting for the *New Republic*, decided to find out where the jobless unattached women—the invisible ones—were. She talked to YWCA administrators and welfare groups, and to the women themselves.

There are many women, no doubt, who struggle along until the last possible moment. Social investigators are almost of a mind that the unemployed woman of the new type is much more reluctant to apply for aid at a public charity than is her brother in similar circumstances. She tries everything else first, for the doctrine of Success has taken strong hold of the public mind, and to admit failure is still the greatest shame of all. She lives as long as possible on her savings, trying all the time to find more work and going without enough food to save money for clothes. Then she turns to her friends—private borrowing is not quite so shameful—until she becomes too much a burden. There are girls who for the past few months have risen every morning before dawn, to be first in the lines of applicants for any job that has been advertised, and when the early-morning rush is over and it is too late to hope for success, they must look for a place to sit, to wait until the day is over. That place is not easy to find, particularly in winter. The railroad-station waiting rooms grew so crowded that now they are kept clear by having the "vagrants" turned out every so often. It is not until she is reduced to actual hunger that the white-collar girl at last presents herself at the door of the relief bureaus and charity committees . . .

Homeless, friendless women are much troubled with their belongings; they cannot trudge the streets and look for work if they are burdened by their bundles and suitcases. Some solve the problem by simply deserting their possessions; they move late at night from the rooms for which they cannot pay, leaving everything they own in default of rent money . . .

Certainly at the moment there are far too many trained women for every type of work. The business colleges have gone on turning out typists, file-clerks and accountants at an increasing rate of speed, though new labor-saving office machinery is always being invented. The untrained factory worker has lost her high social position in comparison with the housemaids and cooks who used to demand enormous wages in compensation for their menial tasks. Many women are now going into jobs as cooks or maids at ridiculously low wages, for the advantage of a place to live and the certainty of regular meals. At least one college-bred woman is in New Jersey now, earning six dollars a week as a cook . . .

Half-time jobs. Temporary jobs. Free meals in restaurants that have come to the fore and offered their left-over food. Free rooms in hotels that cannot fill themselves otherwise. Failing these makeshift devices, emptiness lies before the woman who has no claim on the relief usually afforded the deserving "case," the unwed mother or the blind and decrepit. So far, the unattached woman has got the leavings, not only of charity. Even now, when it

A drawing from the 1930s sketchbook of artist Raphael Soyer.

would seem they had reached rock-bottom, the greater number of these homeless drifters have not come to public attention. One by one they give up, slowly and reluctantly, or they go too far even to give up, like the fifty-year-old woman who confessed: "I had $60, but I spent it. I didn't even try to save it. I thought perhaps God would be good to me and let me die."

Goin' Down the Road

I'm goin' down the road feel-in' bad,___ I'm__ goin' down the road feel-in' bad,___ I'm goin' down the road feel-in' bad, Lord, Lord,__ And I ain't gonna be treat-ed this-a-way.___

· 2 ·

I'm lookin' for a job with honest pay,

· 3 ·

Two-dollar shoes hurt my feet,

· 4 ·

But ten-dollar shoes fit 'em neat,

· 5 ·

I'm goin' where the water tastes like wine,

· 6 ·

Forty cents an hour won't pay my rent,

· 7 ·

I can't live on cornbread and beans,

· 8 ·

I'm goin' down the road feelin' bad,

★ | 5 | ★

WANDERING

The deepest wounds of the depression were borne by children. Years of poverty, hunger, and disillusionment piled a weight of suffering on shoulders too young to bear it. It was as concrete as the fact that, according to *Outlook* magazine in 1932, "Mr. and Mrs. Joseph Jacobs of New York City have decided to name their new-born baby girl Norma Depression Jacobs."

Here are a young boy's impressions:

The first hard times I remember came in 1933, when I was in the eighth grade. Travis and Son shut down and for six months Dad didn't draw a penny. Things must have been pinching for two or three years before that because by that time the house was mortgaged and the money spent. I don't know much about the details. . . .

Then we were really up against it. For a whole week one time we didn't have anything to eat but potatoes. Another time my brother went around to the grocery stores and got them to give him meat for his dog—only he didn't have any dog. We ate that dog meat with the potatoes. I went to school hungry and came home to a house where there wasn't any fire. The lights were cut off.

They came out and cut off the water. But each time, as soon as they left, my brother went out and cut it on again with a wrench.

I remember lying in bed one night and thinking. All at once I realized something. We were poor. Lord! It was weeks before I could get over that. . . .

We lost our car and house and kept moving from one house to another. Bill collectors hunted us down and came in droves. Every now and then my brother or Dad would find some sort of odd job to do, or the other brother in Chicago would send us a little something. Then we'd go wild over food. We'd eat until we were sick. We'd eat four times a day and between meals. We just couldn't help ourselves. The sight and smell of food sort of made us crazy, I guess.

Undernourishment was common throughout the country. Infants and children, in the growing years when good food and decent shelter and a sense of security are of the greatest importance, faced the specter of famine. A big drop in the consumption of milk was noticed in state after state. Everywhere health officials reported that child welfare and public nursing were usually the first services to suffer when city and state budgets were cut.

In Chicago a school principal testified in January 1932: "I said to the teachers last fall, 'Whenever you have a discipline case, ask this question first, What has he had for breakfast?' Which usually brings out the fact that he has had nothing at all." Another gave this testimony:

I shall give you one instance. We were practicing for a chorus and a little boy about twelve years old was in the

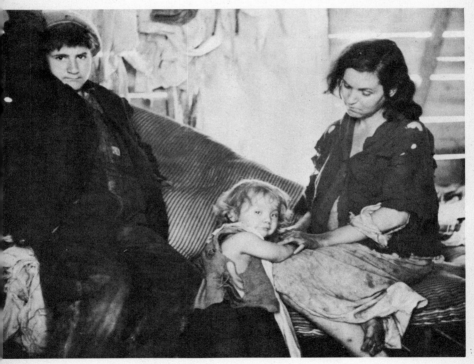

*These children lived with their mother
in a one-room hut built atop a Ford chassis
junked on Highway 70 in Tennessee.*

front line. He was clean in his overalls, but didn't have very much on under them. He was standing in the line when all at once he pitched forward in a dead faint. This was two o'clock in the afternoon. When he was revived, I tried to find the cause and he said he was hungry. He had not had anything to eat since the day before.

Education was crippled. The funds to pay for it came out of local taxes. As incomes dropped in the early years of the depression, tax revenues shrank. In small towns and big cities budget cutters made the public schools their victims. Plans for new buildings were shelved. The knife cut textbooks, equipment, salaries. Teachers were fired, and fifty pupils were crowded into rooms designed to hold thirty. The school year was clipped short, sometimes down to six or seven months. Departments were dropped and special services slashed.

In some places schools survived only because the teachers made the sacrifice. Salaries were cut as much as 50 percent. In rural areas some teachers were paid as little as $280 for an eight-month school year. Often teachers would get not money, but promises to pay later; but still they went on teaching.

Some teachers and students tried to protest. In Chicago, 14,000 teachers were desperate after almost two years of doing with but a few weeks' pay. In April 1933 the *New York Times* reported from Chicago:

Patience has reached its end. Morale has broken down. Discipline has become extremely difficult. The Board of Education last Wednesday considered a resolution to close the schools. Only the fact that the Spring vacation begins April 27 prevented its passage. Only the threat that, by striking, the teachers would forfeit their pension rights and their civil service standing has thus far prevented the closing of the schools by a general walkout.

That week 15,000 high school pupils struck to back their teachers' cry for help. (Many teachers, hungry and threadbare themselves, had somehow managed to find bread or a pair of shoes for their students.) Thousands of unpaid teachers stormed Chicago's City Hall to demand their back pay, and with pupils and parents paraded their picket signs through the Loop. They invaded several banks, disrupting business, to insist that bankers lend the city money to pay teachers' salaries. Regiments of police, on foot and on horse, moved in and, as one reporter said, "in a moment unpaid policemen were cracking their clubs against the heads of unpaid schoolteachers."

As early as 1930 the census revealed that over 3 million children seven to seventeen years old were not in school. Soon, in Alabama five out of six schools were shut down for lack of funds. Over 300 schools in Arkansas were open only sixty days during the year. In the hard-hit coal state of West Virginia, 1,000 schools gave up altogether and turned their pupils away. New York City laid off 11,000 teachers in 1932–33. By the end of 1933 it was nationwide: 2,600 schools had closed their doors. The education of at least 10 million children was disabled by shutdowns or shortened terms.

At least a third of the children reported out of school by the 1930 census were working—in factories, canneries, farms, or sweatshops in the home. Parents were desperate to see anyone in the family earning and sent their children to work. As a result, sweatshops were springing up everywhere. Back again, as in the earliest years of the Industrial Revolution, were the abuses of long hours, low wages, and unhealthy working conditions. Child labor laws were being openly flouted.

From *I Am a Woman Worker*, a book of autobiographical sketches, comes this account by a fourteen-year-old girl who, during the early Thirties, worked as a seamer in a knitting factory:

This is my daily program.

At 5:30 it is time for me to get up. I am tired and sleepy. After I get up, I hurriedly eat my breakfast, and I am ready to go to work. It is a chilly winter morning, but I know that it will be hot in the mill. I start on my three-mile walk to the factory. As I walk, I see others hurrying to work. I look at the older people and wonder if they, too, feel the resentment every morning that I do, or if as the years go by their spirits are deadened.

I arrive at the factory. The sight that I dread to see meets my eyes: the line of unemployed people waiting for the boss to come and hoping for work.

As I open the door, a force of hot stuffy air greets me. I rush to my machine, as all the girls do, to get ready, so that when the whistle blows we can start working. When doing piece work, every minute counts.

I seam men's heavy underwear. After I finish twelve union suits, I get a check for 6 cents for size fifty, and 4½ cents for the smaller sizes. At the end of the week, I paste my checks in a book and give the book to the boss, who pays according to the number of checks I have. After I finish a dozen union suits, I tie them up and carry them to the bin. The dozens are heavy, and grow heavier as the day goes on. The bin is usually full, and as I throw my dozen up on the top it very often comes down on me. Of course I fall. . . .

Nothing much has happened today. My machine has broken twice, and because the machinist has not been very busy, I have had to wait only about three-quarters of an hour. After my many trips to the bin for my work, and after finishing each dozen, tying it up, signing my number on the check, then carrying it to the next bin, I am so tired that my body and mind grow numb. To arouse myself, I go to the ladies' room. The toilet does not flush very well, but it never does anyway. When I come to the water fountain, no matter how tired and numb I may feel, I am always angry and disgusted. The water is lukewarm; the fountain is rusty and filthy. But my trip to the fountain serves as a stimulant because I am always glad to get back to my bench.

As usual, half of my lunch has been spoiled. I can either put it on the table where I keep my work and where it becomes squashed, or I can put it in a box under my bench and give the rats the first choice.

After a monotonous afternoon, it is almost time to go home. We have three minutes to put our coats on; then we wait in our respective aisles. All eyes are on the boss, waiting for the signal. Then we rush out.

Thousands of other children worked in agriculture, most of them in the families of sharecroppers, black or white; or in migratory farm families, handling the big commercial crops in fruits and berries, tobacco and beets, and truck farming.

Many boys and girls who failed to find jobs near home or felt they were a burden to their parents simply took to the road. A sight new to the 1930s was the army of young transients. The Children's Bureau estimated that by late 1932 a quarter of a million under the age of twenty-one were roaming the country. They hopped freights, bummed their food, and lived along the tracks with the hardened hoboes in squatters' camps called jungles.

Investigating the "vast, homeless horde," *Fortune* magazine found that many had been to high school, some to college. How were the young wanderers treated by America? *Fortune* reported:

Atlanta, a natural way station of the hobo route in the South, gives thirty-day sentences in the city stockade or the chain gang—both of which are filled with degenerates—to anyone caught on a freight train within Fulton County. For this reason the city is widely stigmatized by tramps. Yet 6,000 wandering boys were listed there through September, 1932.

Miami is friendly but firm. The city provides the wanderer with a bathing suit and the unescorted freedom of its famous beach. Afterwards the vagrant is deported. Each day the so-called Hobo Express deposits eight or nine boys at the north line of the county with the warning that return will mean six months of road work. At New Orleans the transient swing to the South becomes the swing to the West. A study of welfare, police, and rail-

road records suggests that 5,000 wanderers traverse the city monthly, most of them under age, with only 500 seeking out the city's highly organized relief organizations. Houston reports a similar passage. Kansas City estimates a daily arrival of 700 youths on freight trains, the departure of the same number, plus the daily passage of 300 automobile hitch-hikers. From June to August last year 504 wandering boys registered with the East St. Louis Salvation Army. Des Moines accommodated 3,000 in 1931. Los Angeles suspects a monthly visitation from 11,000. And so on.

One of the "wild boys of the road," Robert Carter, a Virginian, kept a diary on his wanderings through the South. From it come these notes on boys going nowhere:

Greenville, N.C. Arrived here on a freight train late at night, tired and dirty from train smoke and cinders. I slept in the tobacco warehouse with two other young tramps, one having a suitcase crammed with dirty clothes and a blanket smelling of antiseptic. Next morning was cold, the wind hinted of winter. Leaving town I turned due south, walking the roads. All day I went steadily, getting an occasional ride from trucks or Fords. When dinnertime came I asked for work at a farmhouse for food and picked peas with the farmer's family for two hours.

That night I pried open a church window and slept there. . . .

Charleston, S.C. Traveled across country for days, living as usual, always on the lookout for food, a place to sleep and possible work.

Charleston is full of homeless boys from the North and Northwest, brought by the delusion of palm trees and warm days. . . .

I slept two nights in the Red Star Mission . . . Slept the third night in the Charleston jail. The cops searched my clothes for weapons, my legs for knives, or perhaps for shackles, and showed me a bench hardly a foot wide to sleep on. The night was hot, the bench an impossible place and the mosquitoes were swarming. . . .

En Route. Grabbed a freight towards Macon. Boys were scattered all over the train, with fifteen or twenty in the box-car I was in. Some lay sleeping on old paper, others swapped yarns, passed on recipes, told each other of bad detectives, of good places and friendly people, and where to catch the trains in and out of big towns. One, a boy of twenty, was just off the chain gang and showed us his leg raw from the shackles . . .

Macon, Ga. We descended on Macon in a horde and were swallowed up by the streets. Yet we were there, dozens of us, bumming the same houses and restaurants, wandering the same streets, vague and lonely, ever on the move.

That night I slept in the Salvation Army. It was crowded with boys and young men, some with small grips, others with nothing but the shirts on their backs. One boy, a nightmare of rags and dirt, was so thin and far-gone that we tramps, ourselves destitute, gave him of our stock of goods. . . .

En Route. Leaving Macon I am the only one on the freight to Atlanta. Perhaps there are others, for this line has a bad name and we may be hiding from each other. That night I rode an oil tank and as the night was cold I stood up, holding the railing with rigid hands and staring ahead, watching the smoke grow red when the firemen stoked the boiler. I tied my bundle to the railing for fear of losing it, and stamped my feet to keep from dozing. But I slept in spite of myself. When I awoke with a jerk, I found myself leaning far over the gulf of grinding wheels. I was too frightened to sleep during the rest of the night. . . .

En Route. Leaving Atlanta with three other boys, youngsters going deeper South, we were rounded up in the railroad yards by five detectives carrying pistols and shotguns. They caught eighteen or twenty of us after beating the bushes about the yards. They herded us to a bank beside the railroad, all of us young, none over twenty-five except a middle-aged man looking for a place by some river to jungle-up for the winter. They examined us for scars from shackles, threatened us with three months on the chain gang. . . .

Chattanooga, Tenn. Finally got into Tennessee, tired, dispirited and hopeless. I decided to go to Mexico or California. It didn't matter.

At one crossing in this town fully a hundred men and boys had gathered and were waiting for the southbound freight. When the train came the boys issued from the grass, from junk piles, from the shadows of nearby houses, and began to swing on the train as it passed the crossing.

Some had packs, some tattered suitcases, others had bundles or nothing at all.

The song "Wandering" described their way of life:

Wandering

There's fish in the ocean, there's eels in the sea,
But a red-headed woman made a fool out of me,
And it looks like I'm never going to cease my wandering.

I've been working in the army, I've been working on a farm,
And all I've got to show is the muscle in my arm,
And it looks like I'm never going to cease my wandering.

Ashes to ashes and dust to dust,
If the Republicans don't get you, the Democrats must,
And it looks like I'm never going to cease my wandering.

O, I've been wandering far and wide,
I come with the wind, I drift with the tide,
And it looks like I'm never going to cease my wandering.

THE PROMISED CITIES

For the black American, poverty had been chronic ever since Emancipation. He was "the first man fired and the last man hired," the saying went. It was no different in the Great Depression. A black social worker, Anna Arnold Hedgeman, described what happened in Harlem in the early Thirties in her autobiography, *The Trumpet Sounds:*

> With the financial collapse in October 1929, a large mass of Negroes were faced with the reality of starvation and they turned sadly to public relief. A few chanted optimistically, "Jesus will lead me and the Welfare will feed me," but others said it was a delusion, for the Home Relief Bureau allowed only eight cents a meal for food. Meanwhile men, women and children combed the streets and searched in garbage cans for food, foraging with dogs and cats.
>
> The crashing drop of wages drove Negroes back to the already crowded hovels east of Lenox Avenue. In many blocks one toilet served a floor of four apartments. Most of the apartments had no private bathrooms or even the luxury of a public bath. Where a tub could be found, it usually had been installed in the kitchen. All of these

tenements were filthy and vermin-ridden. There were flats with old-fashioned toilets which rarely flushed, and when they did, overflowed on the floors below. In the winter gaping holes in the skylights allowed cold air to sweep down the staircase. Coal grates provided the only heat. The tenants scoured the neighborhood for fuel, and harassed janitors in the surrounding districts were compelled to stand guard over coal deliveries until they were safely stored in the cellars. . . .

Many families had been reduced to living below street level. It was estimated that more than ten thousand Negroes lived in cellars and basements which had been converted into makeshift flats. Packed in damp, rat-ridden dungeons, they existed in squalor not too different from that of the Arkansas sharecroppers. Floors were of cracked concrete, and the walls were whitewashed rock, water-drenched and rust-streaked. There were only slits for a window and a tin can in a corner was the only toilet.

Shunted into these run-down sections, Negroes were forced to pay exorbitant rents to landlords who flagrantly violated the city building and sanitary codes. Compared with the 20 to 25 per cent of their income white families generally paid for rent, Negro tenants paid from 40 to 50 per cent. More than half the Negro families were forced to take in lodgers to augment the family income. Frequently, whole families slept in one room. Envied was the family who had a night worker as a lodger, for he would occupy a bed in the day that would be rented out at night, same room, same bed, same sheets and same bedbugs. This was described as the "hot bed." If the family had a bathtub, it, too, was covered with boards and rented out.

A street scene in Harlem during the Thirties.

By the time of the crash, 40 percent of America's blacks were living in ghettos in the cities. They had been moving up from the South for the past fifteen years. The boll weevil, invading Southern cotton fields, had started the migration. By 1915 the insect had ruined vast acres of land, and much of what was left was devastated by flood and drought. Black sharecroppers and field hands, cut off from credit, hungry and cold in their rickety cabins, had no place to turn.

Except North. That way lay the promise of jobs. The war that had started in Europe in 1914 had blocked the tide of emigrants to America. Factories in the North, prospering on war orders, were looking for labor. Blacks streamed North to realize the dream of good jobs, good homes, good schools. By 1920 half a million had come. They found jobs in most industries, and ten years later the number of migrants had swelled to a million and a quarter. Chicago, Detroit, Cleveland, New York, Philadelphia—they were meccas. But now the promised cities proved almost as cruel as the Jim Crow South.

Of all those thrown out of work by the crash, proportionately more blacks than whites lost their jobs. The percentage of jobless blacks sometimes ran four, five, or six times higher. In 1930, 15.7 percent of blacks were unemployed, against 9 percent of whites; in 1931, 35 percent of blacks were jobless, 24.1 percent of whites; in 1932, 56 percent of blacks, 39.7 percent of whites.

Why? In most places whites received preference when jobs were scarce. But worse, a tendency to replace black workers with white was soon seen. White girls, for instance, replaced black waiters, hotel employees, and elevator operators—all at reduced rates.

In Chicago, wrote Mauritz Hallgren in his book, *Seeds of Revolt,* "I had found the suffering among the jobless . . . immeasurably worse than in any other section or city. This was especially true of the Negroes. One could go into home after home along Dearborn Street, State Street, and Wabash Avenue, between Thirty-fifth and Fifty-first Streets, and find not a single scrap of food."

Visiting Chicago in 1932, novelist and critic Edmund Wilson explored an old tenement building housing sixty-seven Negro families:

The Angelus Building looms blackly on the corner of its block: seven stories, thick with dark windows, caged in a dingy mesh of fire-escapes like mattress-springs on a junk-heap, hunched up, hunchback-proportioned, jam-crammed in its dumbness and darkness with miserable wriggling life.

It was built in 1892 and was once the Ozark Hotel, popular at the time of the old World's Fair. In the dim little entrance hall, the smudged and roughened mosaic, the plaster pattern of molding, the fancy black grill of the elevator, most of it broken off, do not recall former splendor—they are abject, mere chips and shreds of the finery of a section now dead, trodden down into the waste where they lie. There is darkness in the hundred cells: the tenants cannot pay for light; and cold: the heating system no longer works. It is a firetrap which has burned several times—the last time several people were burned to death. And, now, since it is not good for anything else, its owner has turned it over to the Negroes, who flock into the tight-

packed apartments and get along there as best they can on such money as they collect from the charities.

There are former domestic servants and porters, former millhands and stockyard workers; there are prostitutes and hoodlums next door to respectable former laundresses and Baptist preachers. One veteran of the war, once foreman of the Sunkist Pie Company, now lives in cold and darkness with his widowed mother, even the furniture which he had been buying for $285 the outfit and on which he had paid all but the last installment of $50.20, taken away by the furniture company. For light, they burn kerosene lamps, and for warmth, small coal-stoves and charcoal buckets. The water-closets do not flush, and the water stands in the bathtub.

The children go to play in the dark halls or along the narrow iron galleries of an abysmal central shaft, which, lighted faintly through glass at the top, is foggy and stifling with coal-smoke like a nightmare of jail or Hell. In the silence of this dreadful shaft, sudden breakages and bangs occur—then all is deathly still again. The two top floors have been stripped by fire and by the tenants' tearing things out to burn or sell: apartments have lost their doors and plumbing pipes lie uncovered. These two floors have been condemned and deserted. Relief workers who have visited the Angelus Building have come away so overwhelmed with horror that they have made efforts to have the whole place condemned—to the piteous distress of the occupants, who consider it an all-right-enough place when you've got nowhere else to go. And where to send these sixty-seven Negro families?

Despite such conditions, many more Negroes moved North during the depression decade, for in the rural South they were facing starvation and terror. Jobs were sometimes being seized from blacks by violence. Newspaper-columnist Marquis W. Childs reported in February 1930:

In southwest Missouri there was recent evidence of a condition that is probably aggravating the situation in many rural areas. A Negro schoolhouse was burned at Grayridge, in Stoddard County, and a merchant in the town received a threatening note, warning him to discharge the Negro employees on his farm. The sheriff of the county explained that several such threats had been received. He believed the anonymous letters came from white farm hands who had left the community for better pay in the city five or six years before and now were returning, out of work and broke, to demand their old jobs back.

Hilton Butler, writing for the New Republic, said, "In 1929, before the crash, people generally were in a fairly good and unsuspecting humor. In 1930 the depression invaded everything from Broadway to the R.F.D.'s. Tempers grew short and ugly, restlessness demanded an outlet, and lynchings nearly doubled."

Butler also investigated reports that black firemen on the railroads in Mississippi were even being shot because white railroadmen wanted their jobs. He wrote:

Frank Kincaid, Negro fireman on the Mississippi division of the Illinois Central Railroad, climbed into the cab of "The Creole" as crews were being changed late one night in Canton, twenty-five miles north of Jackson, the

This tenement on Chicago's South Side was photographed by Russell Lee.

capital of Mississippi. Against the lighted window he made a perfect target for a gunman in the darkness outside. A shotgun belched a load of buckshot into the Negro's head and he fell back into the coal tender to die. A white man took his place, and "The Creole" pulled out for New Orleans. . . .

Ed Cole, a Negro fireman on the same division, stepped at night from his cab to throw a switch at Water Valley junction. From behind the curtains of an unlighted automobile that drew up beside the track a shotgun roared, and Ed fell over the switch to die. A white man took his place in the cab.

Mississippi, in its own primitive way, had begun to deal with the unemployment problem. Dust had been blown from the shotgun, the whip, and the noose, and Ku Klux practices were being resumed in the certainty that dead men not only tell no tales but create vacancies.

By early 1933 it was verified that in Mississippi seven Negro railroad workers had been murdered, seven had been wounded, and one flogged. But no one was ever indicted or convicted for the murders.

Justice? No, murder was not news in Mississippi, and the killing of a black by a white rarely reached the courts, or even a newspaper.

Over 300,000 Negroes migrated from the South in the 1930s. Although it was less than half the number that had gone North in the previous decade, it raised the black population in the big northern centers by 23 percent.

★ 7 ★

MIDDLE-CLASS BLUES

What happened to the middle class in the depression?

Walking the streets of Lowell, Massachusetts, in 1930, Louis Adamic saw how badly its small businessmen were doing.

Every third or fourth store in the main streets was vacant. There were few "For Rent" signs in the windows, the proprietors figuring, I suppose, that it was no use putting them up. One sign read: "For Rent at Your Own Price."

In the main business section, the five-and-ten-cent store seemed to be the only really busy place. A butcher told me that he sold few steaks and chops; most of the customers bought tripe, soup bones and the cheaper cuts of meat. He had ordered but a few turkeys for Thanksgiving. Grocery and dry-good prices were at least one-third lower in Lowell than in New York or Boston, but even so the stores were doing little business. Two merchants confessed they were operating at a loss; they were "caught"; people owed them money for years back, and they were hoping "things would pick up soon." Said one shopkeeper, "But I don't know how much longer I can hold out on hope."

A barber told me that people obviously were cutting

their hair at home; several barbershops had gone out of business . . .

I spoke with physicians. One admitted that he, like the other doctors in town, had difficulties in collecting his fees; perhaps more than half of his patients were "charity."

Everyone was scrimping. Advertisers that had been extravagant in the 1920s were pennypinchers in the 1930s. This ad, which appeared in the *Saturday Evening Post*, pictured a family of four. The mother was speaking:

FIGURE IT OUT FOR YOURSELF . . . THIS NEW TOOTH PASTE SAVES US A DOLLAR A MONTH AND GIVES US BRIGHTER TEETH.

We're just an average family—mother, father, and two children. And tooth paste takes up such a small part of our budget, that we never stopped to think of making any real savings on it.

But money's been getting so scarce with us lately we've had to get the utmost value out of every dollar. So I was mighty interested to see that the Listerine people made a tooth paste for half the usual price. . . .

I figured out the savings it would give us. We use a tube a month. We had been buying a 50¢ tooth paste, spending $2 a month for the family. Now that we've switched to Listerine Tooth Paste, we save a dollar every month. And that gave me an idea of how to go about saving on other things we need.

The ad went on to suggest what could be bought with a yearly savings of three dollars per person in a family of four:

7 lbs. steak, 8 lbs. bacon
10 lbs. ham, 8 lbs. lamb chops
2 chickens, a large roast
12 jelly rolls, coffee rings,
        cheese cakes or angel cakes
6 qts. olive oil, 20 quarts milk
100 oranges, 20 lbs. lard
150 lbs. prunes, 60 lbs. sugar
36 packages rice, 15 lbs. coffee
3 lbs. tea, 30 loaves bread

It did not usually work so well. Some estimates held that more than half the 16 million people reported unemployed in the spring of 1933 belonged to the lower middle class. Social workers had noticed a pattern in their makeshift. First they went through their cash savings, then insurance policies were dropped, jewelry and clothes were pawned, and the furniture sold. Then bills at the grocery store could no longer be paid, and sometimes the family would move into a poorer neighborhood. Often it meant the painful loss of a house partly paid for. In 1932 about 273,000 families lost their homes through foreclosure. Early the next year a thousand homes a day were being taken over by mortgage holders.

In business, it was the independent merchant, the small manufacturer, and the small banker who collapsed or was swallowed up by the giant operators. The retail chains and the mail-order houses did not fail, nor did such corporations as U.S. Steel or General Motors, though their profits dropped sharply. By the end of 1933 altogether 85,000 businesses had failed, with losses of $4.5

Unable to pay rent, the jobless were often evicted,
with their belongings tossed out on the street,
as in this Chicago scene.

billion. Professionals who were self-employed lost clients or patients. Some who worked for others were fired, or their salaries were slashed.

By July 1, 1932, stockholders had lost $74 billion from the fall in stock values. In March of that year the magazine *Outlook* had offered them an imaginative solution:

A method of escaping from the depression has been revealed to us. It seems that Wanamaker's is selling all sorts of frozen meats, fish, fruits, and vegetables. A gent named Birdseye discovered how to freeze them so they'd keep for months. While fishing in the Arctic he noticed that the fish froze as soon as they were taken from the water, but that upon being thrown into a bucket of warm water they not only thawed, but actually returned to life. . . .

Why wouldn't a person do the same thing? Why couldn't you engage a room in a cold storage plant, then arrange with your bank or trust company to take you down to the refrigerating plant, get you frozen, put you in storage, and then, say when steel gets back to 100, go down and get you and throw you into a tub of hot water? . . .

We believe it's a perfectly workable scheme. And if a lot of people did it, it would give the bankers raison d'être, too.

By the fall of 1932 over 6,000 banks—about one fourth of the country's total—had closed their doors. Nine million people who believed their cash had been safely stored deep inside steel vaults saw it disappear overnight. What was now "as good as money in the bank," if banks could collapse? The shock left people thinking there was nothing they could believe in.

One such stunned town, a small midwestern place of 19,000, which he concealed under the name of Melrose, was visited by Marquis W. Childs in the winter of 1932–33. The columnist saw "the recurrent phenomena of the depression, empty stores, For Rent signs, smokeless factories, closing-out sales." In the prosperous Twenties the game had been to find out how much your neighbor was spending; now, he said, it was to find out how much he had lost:

The collapse of the banks and the bonds the bankers sold was the immediate cause of the deflation in Melrose. School teachers, insurance salesmen, small wage earners, dentists, retired farmers, saw life savings disappear, security vanish. An entire generation, with striking exceptions, has been stripped. . . .

The First National Bank of Melrose was the first to go. There was no warning; in the middle of the banking day the doors were closed by the examiners. It was one of the oldest banks in the state, regarded as a branch of the United States Treasury. Within two or three hours everyone knew of the disaster. Depositors, stunned and disbelieving, gathered in small groups to read the notice on the door. . . .

There was little public lamentation. The most shocking example was old Mrs. Gearman. She beat with her fists upon the closed plate-glass doors and screamed and sobbed without restraint. She had in a savings account the $2,000 from her husband's insurance and $963 she had saved over a period of twenty-five years from making rag rugs. Nothing was left but charity.

George Grosz sketches a park bench with a stock broker, fallen on hard times, fastidiously eating his popsicle between two other victims of the depression.

A BROKER ON VACATION

For professionals who had worked fifteen, twenty, or twenty-five years, what was it like to lose a job? And with a family to worry about? Those who had worked steadily had developed a self-confidence that was like an anesthetic, blocking the first pain of unemployment. They believed in a few weeks word would get around that they were available and offers would come in. But the trusting hopefulness soon turned sour. In the May 13, 1931, issue of the *Nation*, Frank Moorhead, who had lost his job as an editorial writer, told what it felt like to be suddenly "broke at fifty-five":

First, indifference; next, reassuring faith; third, galling bitterness; fourth, morbidity. And the last is what hurts and causes folks to fall out of ten-story windows, accidentally. "Nothing wrong with his accounts; happily married," say the newspapers. How about the rapidly dwindling bank balance; the determination that the loved ones, who were in no way to blame for the bad luck, shall go on having the things they were accustomed to having; the stiff upper lip the grand old Scotch mother used to talk about, before you ever had a penny of your own and were too young to go out in the world and work?

Around fifty a man loses nerve—I don't mean the nerve it takes to accompany Wilkins under the ice to the North Pole, or to fly with Byrd and moving-picture men over the South Pole. I mean the nerve it takes to ask a stranger for a job, when you've turned down thousands of men yourself without batting an eye; to tell a friend how good you are, and watch his face continue blank; to approach the banker whom you puffed in your paper for years and who was only too glad to lend you whatever you wanted at 6 per cent, and not even take the interest out in advance. This time he suggests that the wife sign the note, too, and make it 7 per cent, in advance, and asks for a credit statement.

... I should like to find out at what stage of your poverty other people realize or sense it, and pass you by as one no longer interesting or useful to them. You wear the same suit, more carefully brushed and pressed than ever before to conceal your poverty. You walk just as cockily. You know as much; you know a lot more, in fact—things you didn't suspect or believe before. I guess, after all, it's the droop in the shoulders, the look in your eyes—furtive, expectant, resentful.

The nights are the worst; the time when all you can see is the unseen. You've done everything humanly possible to avert the inevitable. You've gone over your life-insurance policies, to be sure they are all incontestable after the first year. You've taken out additional accident insurance. You realize that for the first time in your rather carefree, indifferent life you are worth more dead than alive—a good deal more.

Most professionals found their skills useless in the job market. Paul ("Doc") Evans, later to be widely known as a jazz musician, was making his living by teaching school when, he recalled:

Finally the depression did catch up with me, and my school teaching job folded. I came up to Minneapolis and found a job playing and it was pretty rugged. I can remember going out on jobs strictly on percentage and making fifty cents or something like that and then I can remember playing jobs where you were guaranteed two dollars. It was pretty rough. . . .

And of course, for a number of those years I had another sideline. I raised cocker spaniels and made part of my income from that. It was a little hard to depend on music entirely. So I raised cockers. It's hard to say when I started, because you sort of sneak into these things. But I raised cockers for six or seven years. And I showed them all over. . . .

It isn't easy to say what the Thirties were. One thing that made them different, I think, was that we did things then that nobody would do now. At Lindy's, now called Augie's, for instance, we'd have a band and it would depend on business how many players we'd have or how long we'd play. Sometimes along in the evening the boss would send half the band home, or keep maybe only the piano and the sax or something like that. Then those of us who had been sent home would walk down the street to another joint or drive up on the North Side and sit in with Negro musicians. One place I remember never hired more than a piano player, and when we were done working we'd go and play with him. We never knew who'd show up. And half the time when we were done playing and would come out on the street it would be bright sunlight.

A college education was scarcely of value. On July 27, 1932, the *New York Times* disclosed that graduates from eastern colleges had formed the Association of Unemployed College Alumni. The group estimated that there were more than 10,000 unemployed alumni in New York City alone. Colleges represented in the association included Harvard, Swarthmore, Vassar, Columbia, New York University, City College, and Hunter.

The economic base of writers and artists is shaky even in normal times. Novelist Erskine Caldwell—whose *God's Little Acre* would be published in 1933—had a hungry family of four to support, and arrived in New York with a dime in his pocket. He slept nights in a hallway while he hunted for work.

Benjamin Appel was an aspiring writer who had just graduated from college. Writing in a special issue of *The Carleton Miscellany* devoted to the Thirties, he told what many artists felt then:

The hungry workingman of the 1930's had no hesitation in griping about what-the-hell's-wrong. The hungry writer echoed him at the typewriter. He felt free because he had no security to speak of, and out of insecurity created a philosophy: to free lance it on beans and hamburger, and above all to steer clear of the easy money. Some of us were grimly or romantically idealistic; some were married to wives with jobs; some itched to "sell out to Hollywood" but alas, never had the opportunity. We lived in cheap flats, working at cheap-pay jobs when we had to as clerks, laborers, millhands, lumberjacks—remember, this was the depression with its own idealized image of the worker who surely would save America! We picketed, we wrote pamphlets, joined committees, signed petitions protesting all sorts of social injustices. And we wrote, rather proud on the whole to be outside the corrupting big money.

Others discovered a new independence in the midst of the depression. They learned to live another—and more joyous—style of life. In the same issue of *The Carleton Miscellany*, a poet, Ruth Lechlitner, told what happened to her and her husband Paul:

So when the depression really struck, and we no longer had steady incomes, we at least owned land and shelter. We were lucky—even though for more than seven lean years we had no electricity or running water, no phone, no heat except from the wood we cut and burned in our pot-belly stove, and some of those winters weren't balmy. But Paul made terraced garden-beds on our hilly slopes to hold what soil we had, scattered between those eternal stones, and we grew our own vegetables and berries. The surplus I canned, pickled and jammed all summer to have for winter use. We found a free supply of apples from un-fenced trees, abundant swamp blueberries, other kinds of wild fruit, and nuts. We started a few chickens for our own use, gradually expanded their number till we had enough eggs to sell a few dozen weekly. Our eggs went also to the village meatmarket to be traded for a few pounds of hamburger or a little bacon (we got awfully tired of eating old hen and rooster) or an occasional precious quarter-pound of butter.

Plain bourgeois rugged individualism. Yeah. It wasn't all duck-soup. But we ate. We wore second-hand clothes given us by friends in the city who still had regular em-ployment. . . .

I'm not starry-eyed about those grim Depression years. But we had fun. We couldn't very often afford the 50-mile train trip to the city, but we had a varied assortment of friends among other young writers who came up for long weekends, happy to sample our home-grown chicken and vegetables. They brought along, when they had the wherewithal, liquid supplement—to help stimulate many a late-hour discussion of our writing problems, and of the times in which we lived.

John Steinbeck, unknown then but later to become a Nobel Prize winner for his novels, was living in California in the early 1930s. He had two assets to carry him through the hard times. His father owned a small cottage in Pacific Grove and let him stay there rent-free. And from the sea the young writer could gather food to eat and driftwood to keep warm. He was part of a group of young people, all poor, and all living the same way.

We pooled our troubles, our money when we had some, our inventiveness and our pleasures. I remember it as a warm and friendly time. Only illness frightened us. You have to have money to be sick—or did then. And dentistry also was out of the question, with the result that my teeth went badly to pieces. Without dough you couldn't have a tooth filled. . . .

Being without a job, I went on writing—books, essays, short stories. Regularly they went out and just as regularly came back. Even if they had been good, they would have come back because publishers were hardest hit of all. When people are broke, the first things they give up are books. I couldn't even afford postage on the manuscripts. My agents, McIntosh & Otis, paid it, although they couldn't sell my work. . . .

Given the sea and the gardens, we did pretty well with a minimum of theft. We didn't have to steal much. Farmers and orchardists in the nearby countryside couldn't sell their crops. They gave us all the fruit and truck we could carry home. We used to go on walking trips carrying our gunny sacks. If we had a dollar, we could buy a live sheep, for two dollars a pig, but we had to slaughter them and carry them home on our backs, or camp beside them and eat them there. We even did that.

Keeping clean was a problem because soap cost money. For a time we washed our laundry with a soap made of pork fat, wood ashes and salt. It worked, but it took a lot of sunning to get the smell out of the sheets.

★ | 8 | ★

HOOVER'S HOTELS

Early in the depression—by the spring of 1930—lines of men seeking shelter were visible on the streets of every American city. Wherever you turned, there was a gray-black snake, waiting and waiting.

In March 1930 reporter Bruce Bliven of the *New Republic* took a look at one of the biggest lines, the line waiting to get into the Municipal Lodging House conducted by the New York City Department of Public Welfare. It was on 25th Street, near the East River. You were not allowed to spend more than five nights there in any one month. In February, 1,100 men, on the average, had sought its shelter each night. During the first two months of 1930 almost 14,000 men were cared for. Bliven wrote:

It seems too cold to rain; but it isn't. The drops come down in slanting lines, driven by a bitter wind, and stand in pools upon the hard-packed, icy snow along the street. A bad night to be out, even if you are well shod and warmly clothed; and most of the men lounging along the Bowery, with the L trains rumbling overhead, are neither. Their shoes are broken, their clothing is in the last stages of disrepute. Perhaps one in twenty has gloves, and perhaps two in five an overcoat of some sort, an overcoat too large or too small, or with the buttons missing so that it has to be held together with one hand, as the great ladies hold their fur wraps going into the opera. Misery does love company; these unhappy men move along the street, or stand huddled in doorways partly out of the rain, in twos and threes. Here and there you will see a born raconteur who has assembled an audience of half a dozen; they laugh noisily when he comes to the point, and that laughter is the only sound they ever make above an undertone. For most of them are frightened, and frightened men keep quiet.

You turn a corner, and here is a surprising spectacle. There is a line of men, three or sometimes four abreast, a block long, and wedged tightly together—so tightly that no passer-by can break through. For this compactness there is a reason: those at the head of this grey-black human snake will eat tonight; those farther back probably won't. Every few minutes, someone tries to break in far enough toward the front to be enumerated among the blessed; and then, from those behind him comes a chorus of hoots and jeers, the human equivalent of automobilists blowing horns in stalled traffic . . .

The Lodging House opens at four in the afternoon and by that time, the line outside the door is the better part of a block long. It will be twice as long by six. One hundred twenty-eight men are admitted about every twenty-five minutes, that being the length of time it takes for one sitting in the dining room. Every man receives a cup of coffee (in a tin cup, boiling hot), a big dish of stew (beef to-

"Breadline," etched by Reginald Marsh in 1932, from the collection of the Museum of Modern Art, New York City.

night and lamb tomorrow) and as much graham bread as he can eat. Anyone capable of consuming a second helping of stew is welcome to it. After supper, they are registered and check their valuables (nine out of ten haven't any, and if by a miracle somebody turned up with three dollars he would be refused admission). Every man hands in all his clothing, to be fumigated during the night and returned to him in the morning. Every man gets a shower bath—compulsory; a clean white nightshirt, and a medical examination. If he needs a doctor's care, he is sent over to Bellevue Hospital; otherwise, he gets a bed in a room with several hundred other men, where he sleeps about eleven hours: and so would you, if you had tramped the streets from dawn to dark and had just had a big hot meal, perhaps your first in several days. The earliest men to come in are the earliest out in the morning. Each process takes several hours, when the city's guests are running above a thousand at a time. Every man gets back his clothing and valuables, the garments fumigated in dry heat, and neither wrinkled nor given any odor by the process. Once clad, they are checked out again, are given a hot breakfast, and sent on their way. A few of the men—less than 10 per cent —are required to do a couple of hours' cleaning work to pay for their lodging; the rest make no payment except the humiliation of accepting charity. . . .

For many of them, of course, that is no payment at all. They don't mind being "pauperized"; they welcome the chance. But there are others who pay dearly. This winter differs from previous ones in the exceptionally high number of men who have never before had this sort of experience, for whom it is a personal tragedy too deep for words.

In the spring of 1931 a census was taken of the home-less men in New York City. A few hundred paid volunteers tracked the depression-driven wanderers, moving from flophouse to Municipal Lodging House to Salvation Army shelter. They tabulated those they found roving about the city with no shelter, no prospect of jobs, no place to stay in the daytime or to sleep at night.

The rough count was that there were about 15,000 homeless men in New York.

Several reporters, some of them among America's most talented writers, wanted to find out what was happening to people who had had job, home, security, and ambition taken away from them. Edmund Wilson went to Chicago in 1932 and gave this account of his trip:

The single men are driven to flophouses. During the last year—September 30, 1931–September 30, 1932—50,000 have registered at the clearing house.

. . . these men eat their chicken-feed and slum amid the deafening clanking of trays and dump the slops in g.i. cans; wait for prize-fights or movies of Tarzan (provided to keep them out of the hands of the Communists or from holding meetings themselves) in so-called "recreation halls," on the walls of which they have chalked up "Hoover's Hotel"—big bare chambers smothered with smoke, strewn with newspapers like vacant lots, smeared like the pavements with phlegm.

Here they sit in the lecture seats, squat on the steps of the platform, stretch out on the floor on old papers. In one room a great wall-legend reminds them: "The Blood of God Can Make the Vilest Clean," and they are routed

Getting coffee-and in a mission flophouse.
The lithograph is by Raphael Soyer,
from the Museum of Modern Art.

to mess through a prayer meeting. When they come back to the recreation hall, they discover that a cheerful waltz has served merely as a bait to draw them to the harangue of an old Cicero policeman who says that he has been saved. They are obliged to send their clothes to be fumigated, and if they are wet with the winter rain, ruined. They herd into steaming showers, the young men still building some flesh on straight frames, the old with flat chests, skinny arms and round sagging bellies; and they flop at last on the army cots or in the bunks in double tiers, where the windows which are shut to keep out the cold keep in the sour smell—men in slit union suits and holey socks, men tattoed with fancy pictures of the emblems of some service they have left—resting their bunioned feet taken out of flattened shoes or flat arches wound around with adhesive tape—lying with newspapers for pillows, their arms behind their heads or with a sheet pulled over their faces or wrapped up in blankets.

The men in the flophouses were marched out in the streets at seven in the morning. The new "men of leisure," without jobs, had a whole day to face. How did they pass the time? Matthew Josephson, a historian who also reported for magazines, interviewed one of the men he had met in the East 25th Street lodging house.

My large, barrel-chested friend Smith told me he always felt weak and a bit sleepy for lack of sufficient food, though the fare he got was "good enough for what you pay for it." Where to go? He and the others liked to promenade about the city and its squares or parks. "The public libraries are a Godsend!" he remarked with feeling. But sometimes, out of fatigue, one fell asleep over a book or magazine and was ejected. Slowly wandering the streets, the unemployed might enjoy all the unreeling film of the city's movement. Lacking small necessaries, especially tobacco, they learned to seek these out; they gathered up cigarette ends or cigar butts from the pavement, as well as discarded newspapers and other rubbish from refuse cans. Finally about half their number, no matter how respectable, eventually began to "ask," that meant to beg, Smith explained. The number of mendicants in the central quarters of the city was now estimated at about six thousand. In the early afternoon the thousands of wandering drones would come creeping back to their soup lines.

There was a song about the soup lines:

Soup Song

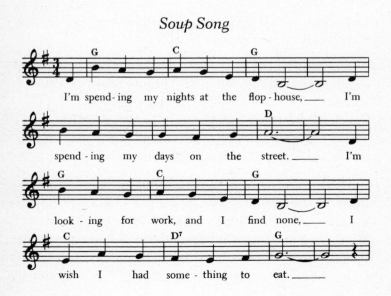

I'm spend-ing my nights at the flop-house, ____ I'm spend-ing my days on the street. ____ I'm look-ing for work, and I find none, ____ I wish I had some-thing to eat. ____

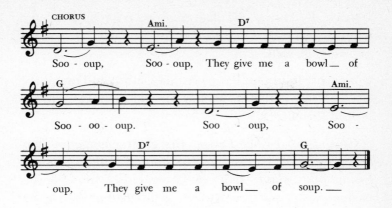

Soo - oup, Soo - oup, They give me a bowl — of Soo - oo - oup. Soo - oup, Soo - oup, They give me a bowl — of soup. —

I spent twenty years in the factory,
I did everything I was told,
They said I was faithful and loyal,
Now even before I get old:
CHORUS

I saved fifteen bucks with my banker
To buy me a car and a yacht,
I went down to draw out my fortune,
And this is the answer I got:
CHORUS

By 1931, for those with a little change in their pockets, restaurants were offering bargains: ALL YOU WANT TO EAT FOR SIXTY CENTS. The *New York Herald Tribune* quoted a restaurant owner describing one man who

"came in Friday night, a rough-looking customer. He had a tomato juice cocktail, soup, three orders of liver with onions and potatoes, two salads, four cups of coffee, a pie a la mode, a custard and some other dessert, a watermelon,

I think. For bread, he had crackers, corn muffins, and whole wheat rolls. I don't think he knew what he was doing when he walked out."

Novelist John Dos Passos visited Detroit and found the city had just closed its shelter for the homeless. He described the effect:

Closing up Fisher Lodge, the giant emergency flophouse conducted in one of the unused buildings of the Fisher Body plant—officially it was closed through lack of money, but actually, I was told on good authority, because the homeless men living there were getting too interested in their forum and the place was getting to be a "nest of Reds"—has turned several thousand workless men out onto the streets and parks of Detroit. They are everywhere, all over the vast unfinished city, the more thrifty living in shacks and shelters along the waterfront, in the back rooms of unoccupied houses, the others just sleeping any place. In one back lot they have burrowed out rooms in a huge abandoned sandpile. Their stovepipes stick out at the top.

All along the wharves and in the ends of the alleys that abut on the waterfront you can see them toasting themselves in the sun, or else patiently fishing. A sluggish, drowsy, grimy life, of which Grand Circus Park is the social center and the One Cent Restaurant operated by some anonymous philanthropist on Woodward Avenue is the Delmonico's. In the evening they stroll up and down Woodward Avenue and look at the posters on the all night movies and cluster around medicine shows and speakers in back lots where you hear the almost forgotten names of old-time labor parties like the Proletarian Party and the Socialist Labor Party.

Unemployment became a way of life, and out of it developed a new style of housing. There was no money for rent. The homeless could make only short stays in the shelters supported by the city or private charity. Unemployed men began to create their own shelters wherever they could find unused land. New York City was soon sprinkled with new settlements. Matthew Josephson described them:

Idle workers congregated in numbers that ran into the thousands in those shantytowns made of tin cans and packing boxes that had sprung up in vacant lots near the river's edge, in the swamps on the New Jersey side of the Hudson, and finally in the "jungle" at the north end of Central Park. These communities were named, in honor of our thrifty President, Hooverville.

In the autumn of 1932 Josephson visited a Hooverville at the foot of East 10th Street on the East River.

It was a fairly popular "development" made up of a hundred or so dwellings, each the size of a dog house or chicken-encoop, often constructed with much ingenuity out of wooden boxes, metal cans, strips of cardboard or old tar paper. Here human beings lived on the margin of civilization by foraging for garbage, junk, and waste lumber. I found some splitting or sawing wood with dull tools to make fires; others were picking through heaps of rubbish they had gathered before their doorways or cooking over open fires or battered oilstoves. Still others spent their days improving their rent-free homes, making them sometimes fairly solid and weatherproof. As they went about their business they paid no attention to curious visitors or the slum children playing underfoot. Most of them, according to the police, lived by begging or trading in junk; when all else failed they ate at the soup kitchens or public canteens. They were of all sorts, young and old, some of them rough-looking and suspicious of strangers. They lived in fear of being forcibly removed by the authorities, though the neighborhood people in many cases helped them and the police tolerated them for the time being.

Between Riverside Drive and the Hudson River, shacks were strung along for two miles. In the spring of 1933 Boris Israel of the *New Republic* went into one, attached to the shore like a barnacle, and talked to the tenant.

Delehanty's house is in the second row from the gap in the fence by which we enter, stooping. For more than twelve years Delehanty was a dyer.

"I'm first from Ireland," he says. "But I'm American, which nobody can deny.". . .

"Thirty years I been in this country," he says, his big, seamed face stuck forward so his strawy hair does not touch the ceiling. "And I fought fer it in the War."

He looks at me from under his great, coarse eyebrows, challenging me to show him what he ever got out of that. We sit and have tea, the lidless kettle sitting precariously on his improvised stove, oven, furnace, hearth of bricks without mortar, the coals glowing hot within. The lamp, slanting from a spike in the wall, gutters full of the oil we got for a nickel I had.

A Hooverville in Brooklyn, New York.

Bill comes in and the small house is almost filled. Dele-hanty's bed takes the whole back end and the battered, shaky table fills one side, leaving room only for some improvised shelves in the corner which hold some rusty tableware, a hatchet, odds and ends, a tomato can half-full of grease for frying, the small bag of sugar I had got for a dime.

"How do you rustle up food?"

"Well, you can get bread out of the bakeries," Delehanty explains. Bill adds, "It's a day or two old, maybe, but it's ok to eat and they can't sell it any more." They explain the round of the small stores, getting food that would rot anyway. "But coffee and sugar, tobacco and oil for the lamps or kerosene for a stove—them's the things that's hard to get," Bill explains. . . .

Only a few years ago Bill was a contractor, in a small way, perhaps, but a contractor. He shows me a picture of his wife and his three-year-old baby boy.

"They're still with her folks," he says. "If I do make any dough I try to send some of it, but hell—"

A HUNK OF BREAD,
A BOWL OF SOUP

Panhandling? It was not the kind of thing an American did, and yet there was not much else to do. For in the early Thirties there was no planned relief, and poverty was considered a disgrace you had only your own shiftlessness to blame for. When the crash of 1929 came, fewer than 200,000 workingmen were able to look to organized unemployment funds for help. (Elsewhere in the world, compulsory unemployment insurance was a reality for 48 million workers.) In many places in the nation relief could be obtained only by signing a pauper's oath. The theory was that if a man wanted to work, he had only to look for a job. Therefore relief should be made as nasty as possible, to force the shiftless to work. At the onset of the depression, relief was in most instances a local responsibility, given with ill-grace and designed to humiliate the needy.

When the crash occurred and unemployment began to swell, President Hoover expected private philanthropy to cope with the unemployment problem. Not until October 1930 did he make a gesture toward the unemployed.

He appointed a President's Emergency Committee for Employment, headed by Colonel Arthur Woods. Its goal was to urge industry to create jobs. It failed, and in the summer of 1931, with a presidential campaign only a year off, Hoover appointed another committee, called the President's Organization on Unemployment Relief. Almost the only thing it did was run advertisements in such places as the *Saturday Evening Post* showing a healthy, smiling worker saying as he tightened his belt, "I'll see it through if you will."

Later, when a Senate committee tried to find out what else the President's Organization had done, its director, Walter Gifford (also President of American Telephone and Telegraph), was obliged to admit that he did not know, nor did his organization know, how many people were out of work or in need of assistance in the United States. He did not even know how many were receiving relief at that time.

Will Rogers, the popular sage and humorist from Oklahoma, observed:

It's almost been worth this depression to find out how little our big men know.

Maby this depression is just "normalcy" and we don't know it.

It's made a dumb guy as smart as a smart one.

Why don't everybody try to make a living out of the conditions we got instead of waiting to make it under conditions that are supposed to come. Suppose "good times" don't never come? Will these manufacturers still hold their stuff at the same price till it does?

Depression used to be a state of mind. Now it's a state of coma, now it's permanent.

Last year we said, "Things can't go on like this," and they didn't, they got worse.

Hoover had earned a large reputation as the "great humanitarian" during World War I because of his record as relief administrator in Europe. Then he had not minded bringing funds and food to hungry Europeans. That presidents before him had not taken strong government action either, during previous economic slumps, set some precedent. But it seemed a paradox that Hoover, who was also a Quaker, now stood firm on the principle that the American government must not give doles.

To those who were well off before the crash and who were relatively untouched by it, Hoover's policy made sense. Some of the new rich and the wilder speculators were ruined by the crash, but it hardly nicked the old money. The great American fortunes accumulated in the nineteenth century stood solid. The paper value of a wealthy family's securities diminished, but the family still owned significant and usually controlling shares in the productive power of America.

While business in general did not grow in the 1930s, some of the great empires managed to expand: U.S. Steel, Western Electric, Du Pont, Standard Oil, Gulf Oil, Shell Oil, Armour, Monsanto Chemical, General Motors. When stock market values fell, the giant corporations bought up more properties at bargain prices.

It is a myth that multimillionaires hurled themselves out of windows in droves when the market broke.

Life

"With this depression on, Maria, I s'pose we ought to go out tonight and consume something."

Actually, some of them, such as Albert Wiggin, Chairman of the Board of Chase National Bank, and George Washington Hill, President of the American Tobacco Company, continued to pay themselves huge salaries and bonuses. Other business leaders were able to maneuver their investments to avoid paying any income tax at all.

Depression or not, the wealthy still went to Bar Harbor on the Maine coast for the summer and to Bermuda for the winter. Those with a taste for musical comedy saw the "Scandals," with Rudy Vallee, and Ethel Merman singing "Life Is Just a Bowl of Cherries." Well-to-do wives still took notice of expensive Paris fashions, such as these advertised in the *New York Times:*

LANVIN ILLUSTRATES
THE NEW ELBOW PUFF IN SLEEVES
Her Jacket in Bright Red Lyons Velvet.
The Low Self-Collar Is Also Important.

NAVY BLUE SKIRT
WITH CAPELET OF LIGHTER BLUE CREPE
and Vestee Inserts of White Angelskin
Affords a Good Example of the Color Contrast
of Which Paris Talks So Much.

But now the wealthy became more conscious of the great gulf between themselves and the millions in poverty. They were less likely to go in for conspicuous display, and big business hired public-relations counselors in an attempt to restore the good will and confidence in their corporations that the public was rapidly losing. A few of

A 1930 advertisement aimed at those who could still afford a weekend at the country club.

the rich—such as "Lady Bountiful," who fed 2,000 to 3,500 men daily on the Bowery for a short while—showed their good intentions. And sometimes they gave benefits, of a sort, for the unemployed. The *New York Daily News* of November 23, 1931, reported:

BOILED NEWPORT BOSOMS TO CUDDLE GREASED PIG
Society in evening clothes chasing a greased pig for the sake of charity will be the usual sight here on Thanksgiving night. . . .
Promptly at midnight a well-greased porker will be released among the meticulously groomed and stiff-shirted gathering. At the expense of clothes and dignity the guests will be expected to wrestle with the oiled animal.

Most of the press adopted the position that business was simply suffering from lack of confidence and that the way to make their readers confident again was to print very little news about the depression and what it was doing to people.

It was taking America a very long time to face the facts of the depression, but by the spring of 1933 some estimates were being made. The figures on unemployment ranged from 13 million to well over 16 million. One fourth of the nation—men, women, and children—belonged to families with no regular income. And the truth was, almost nobody was willing, or prepared, to provide relief to them, certainly not on anything like the scale required.

Little relief came directly from employers. Businessmen were strongly opposed to any measures that would boost the federal income tax still further and would pass on to the owners of industry their proper share of the relief burden. Corporations sometimes contributed to charity and paid the local taxes levied for relief. Some of the bigger firms set up loan funds for workers they had laid off. Only a very few companies had their own unemployment insurance systems. And many of the needy themselves agreed with the philosophy of prosperity: they were ashamed to seek relief and ashamed that they had no jobs.

Few cities, counties, or states had well-organized public relief, and they were not prepared to meet the rising need. Many, no matter how goodhearted, were in no position to do so. Only federal funds could rescue them. Or, as Will Rogers suggested, perhaps the federal government itself needed to be rescued:

> You talk about this country being hard up, every place thinks it's worse off than the other. The Red Cross, as usual, is doing heroic work, but it's the people that they can't reach, people that they never heard of, people that are so far back in the woods that the rest of the world has almost forgotten 'em. Those are the ones that I pity in all this depression. I am speaking of the Senate and Congress of these United States.
>
> I want to see a Red Cross relief formed that will go so far back into the underbrush of the hinterland that it will reach this little known but patriotic group.
>
> Then can the Red Cross say, "We have performed our duty."

In Philadelphia, funds for relief ran dry by the spring of 1932. There were 298,000 people out of work, and 55,000 families had been on relief when the last food orders from private funds were met. Each family had been allowed $3.93 a week for food.

New York City had many private welfare agencies and the nation's richest financial resources. But with the largest population, it also had the heaviest load to bear. Private agencies could not carry the staggering burden; bigger programs were needed.

In the spring of 1931, pressed by prominent citizens who disliked the sight of breadlines and beggars on the streets, the New York State legislature passed a bill, signed by Governor Franklin D. Roosevelt, permitting the city to borrow relief funds. By April, New York City was giving part-time work relief to needy people who could prove they were legal residents and voters for at least two years. By 1932 the City Welfare Bureau was giving weekly doles for home relief of $2.39 per couple; families with children got $6.60. Rent money was handed out every other month. Still, the program reached only one fourth of the estimated 390,000 jobless heads of families.

Blacks found they faced discrimination in the distribution of whatever public relief was given. In Harlem, 56 percent of those who had jobs in 1930 had lost them in 1932, but a survey of jobless Harlem families showed 73.4 percent were not getting any relief. When relief was granted, the rates were often lower than for whites. In Jacksonville, blacks on work relief in 1933 received 20 cents an hour; whites received 30 cents. In Miami, the daily relief wage for blacks was $1.25; for whites it was $2.45. In Atlanta, home relief and work relief for blacks was based on a reduction of 50 cents from whatever whites were given for groceries or wages.

Thus, with a nationwide depression there was only sporadic relief. Mauritz Hallgren studied what this meant in the mining towns of Illinois:

Throughout the coal country—in any event, when I was there in the spring of 1932—there was no unemployment relief worthy of the name. What this meant for the coal country was explained in a few words by Mrs. Sophia Poindexter, a member of the Benton Board of United Charities.

"I'll guarantee you," she said, "that there are at least two thousand children here who haven't had a drop of milk in a year." And Benton was a community with a population of less than ten thousand. More than that, Benton had been one of the most prosperous towns, relatively speaking, in the whole coal country. Four hundred families in and near Benton were being cared for by the United Charities, the average expenditure per family being $1.30 a week. The Red Cross, which had eighty additional families of war veterans on its list, did a little better. It provided groceries at the average rate of $3 per family per week. In all, 1,880 children belonged to these families. What were these people being fed? The grocery orders called for flour, lard, beans, salt, and sugar. No milk was provided, whether fresh or canned, and no fruit or vegetables.

But that was in Benton, where there was at least a semblance of organized relief. At Orient, the site of "the largest mine in the world," there was no organized relief. Coello not only had no money and no relief, but except for two men, who found occasional jobs at Zeigler some miles away, not a person in the town was working or had an income of any sort. Only slightly better off were Buckner, Herrin, Logan, Blairsville, Carterville, Marion and other communities I visited. Here the American Friends' Service Committee was providing milk for a few children; there the Red Cross was distributing occasional grocery orders; in one or two towns local relief funds, though pitifully inadequate, were the source of some help. This latter was true of Marion, the seat of Williamson County.

Far across the country in Oklahoma City hundreds of families, unable to maintain homes, had become squatters on the river-bottom section, living in huts, tents, and shacks. The Veterans of Foreign Wars opened a soup kitchen and distributed relief with no questions asked. The city attempted to follow suit with its own soup kitchen and some work relief. In October 1931 Karl Pretshold reported the effort, makeshift at best, for the *Nation*:

With the encouragement of a committee appointed by Governor Murray, several other soup lines were established under loose State supervision. But the management of these soup kitchens became involved in bills, authority, and red tape. Their affairs have not been wholly straightened out yet. When spring came the soup kitchens of the State and that of the veterans also were closed.

With the winter safely weathered, a chamber-of-commerce committee was appointed to "assist the unemployed." The jobless residents of the city were urged to register and were promised help in finding work. Between 7,000 and 8,000 men and women listed themselves as seeking work. After a check had been made to ascertain whether they were "deserving," Jack Owens, popular civic leader, vice-president of the chamber of commerce, and head of one of the local utilities, as head of the committee placed office space and telephones at the disposal of club-women. These clubwomen telephoned householders, asking if they could give work to unemployed persons. Grass cutting, cleaning yards, removal of trash, painting, and the usual sort of "made" work were located.

There were, of course, psychological effects accompanying the way relief was given. A nation was destitute, and yet the individual was still made to feel he was begging for charity. In the May 1932 issue of the *Atlantic Monthly*, Joseph Heffernan wrote of the "descent from respectability":

This is what we have accomplished with our bread lines and soup kitchens. I know, because I have seen thousands of these defeated, discouraged, hopeless men and women, cringing and fawning as they come to ask for public aid. It is a spectacle of national degeneration. That is the fundamental tragedy for America. If every mill and factory in the land should begin to hum with prosperity tomorrow morning, the destructive effect of our haphazard relief measures would not work itself out of the nation's blood until the sons of our sons had expiated the sins of our neglect.

As early as December 1931 it was plain that both private and public charity were hopelessly inadequate to meet the crisis. In such a situation, what happened? Did people starve?

According to the governors of most states, no one was starving in the first years of the depression. In March 1932, Senator Bingham of Connecticut asked the governors whether everyone in their states who wanted food was getting it. Thirty-nine wired back, in essence, "No one is starving." Eight did not reply. Only one, Governor Gifford Pinchot, admitted that thousands in his state of Pennsylvania were "practically" starving.

From his constituents Governor Pinchot had received many letters begging for help. One of them, written late in 1931, read:

Dear Governor Pinchot: I am sending this letter to you and your wife to ask you won't you please come and help me. I have six little children to take care of. I have been out of work for over a year and a half. Am back almost thirteen months and the landlord says if I don't pay up before the 1 of 1932 out I must go, and where am I to go in the cold winter with my children? If you can help me please for God's sake and the children's sakes and like please do what you can and send me some help, will you, I cannot find any work. I am willing to take any kind of work if I could get it now. Thanksgiving dinner was black coffee and bread and was very glad to get it. My wife is in the hospital now. We have no shoes to were; no clothes hardly. Oh what will I do I sure will thank you.

On June 8, 1932, the *Nation* printed this letter from a Kentucky miner:

We had been eating wild greens since January this year, such as Polk salad. Violet tops, wild onions. forget me-not

wild lettuce and such weeds as cows eat as cows wont eat
a poison weeds. Our family are in bad shape childrens need
milk women need nurishments food shoes and dresses—
that we cannot get. and there at least 10,000 hungry
People in Harlan County daily. I know because I am one
off them. . . . I would leave Harlan County if I only had
$6.00 to send my wife and boy to Bristol-Va. and I could
walk away—But I cant clear a dollar per month that Is
why I am here. that why houndreds are here they cant ship
their family's home. But I am Glad we can find a few
wild greens to get. . . . I borrow this postage to send you
this informations.

Out of the hard times began to come songs of protest.
Some were grim and others funny; sometimes people were
laughing to keep from crying. There was a "Depression
Blues" and an "Unemployment Stomp," a "One Dime
Blues" and a "Welfare Blues." One of the best known
was "Beans, Bacon, and Gravy":

Beans, Bacon, and Gravy

I was born long ago, in 1894,
And I've seen many a panic, I will own;
I've been hungry, I've been cold,
And now I'm growing old.
But the worst I've seen is 1932.

REFRAIN:
Oh, those beans, bacon, and gravy,
They almost drive me crazy,
I eat them till I see them in my dreams,
In my dreams;

When I wake up in the morning,
And another day is dawning,
Yes, I know I'll have another mess of beans.

We congregate each morning
At the country barn at dawning
And everybody is happy, so it seems;
But when our work is done
We file in one by one,
And thank the Lord for one more mess of beans.

REFRAIN

We have Hooverized on butter,
For milk we've only water,
And I haven't seen a steak in many a day;
As for pies, cakes, and jellies,
We substitute sow-bellies,
For which we work the county road each day.

REFRAIN

If there ever comes a time
When I have more than a dime
They will have to put me under lock and key,
For they've had me broke so long
I can only sing this song,
Of the workers and their misery.

REFRAIN

✶ 10 ✶

WHICH SIDE ARE YOU ON?

This minin' town I live in
is a sad an' a lonely place,
For pity and starvation
is pictured on every face,
Everybody hungry and ragged,
no slippers on their feet,
All goin' round from place to place
bummin' for a little food to eat.

That was Aunt Molly Jackson, singing her blues about
the way things were in Harlan County, Kentucky, in 1931.
She was from Straight Creek, one of the many creeks of
the upper Cumberland River in whose valleys the mines
lay. A midwife, Aunt Molly had seen thirty-seven babies
die in her arms that winter. They had died of hunger and
sickness, "their little stomach busted open," she said.
Their fathers, asked to dig coal for thirty-three cents a
ton, had joined a union. The mine company had black-
listed them, and the company doctor refused to treat their
children.

Behind the death of Harlan's babies was the sickness
of the coal industry itself. It collapsed in the depression.

Production and prices slumped disastrously. The small operators who made up the industry cut each other's throats to get business from the big coal users—the steel, railroad, and utility corporations. When they lowered prices, they lowered wages (the biggest part of their costs) and drove the miners to starvation.

At thirty cents a ton, digging seven or eight tons a day and working only a day and a half, a miner was lucky to earn five dollars a week.

What happened to miners happened to many who did not lose their jobs: the depression almost destroyed the already waning American labor movement. Organized labor had made some gains during World War I, but each year that followed saw membership drop. From 5 million in 1920 the American Federation of Labor sank to about 3.5 million in 1929. The proportion of all workers organized into unions was lower than it had been a generation earlier, with hardly 10 percent of America's 30 million nonagricultural workers organized.

The depression slashed incomes easily. Under the fierce pressure to beat starvation, wage-and-hour standards disappeared. In very few industries did workers dare resort to strikes. Where there were laws to safeguard labor, employers rarely hesitated to ignore them. The standards and power of the workers were reduced disastrously.

In 1929 the average per capita income from wages and salaries was $1,475. By 1932 it had dropped to $1,119. President Hoover appealed to employers in 1930 not to cut wages. For a brief time they listened. But in October 1931 U.S. Steel slashed wages 10 percent, and General Motors and U.S. Rubber soon followed. With the action of the giant corporations, wage standards fell throughout American industry. Within a year men were working for 10 cents an hour and children for a dollar a week. By the summer of 1932 average weekly earnings of the labor force had declined from $25.03 to $16.73, and its total income had dropped 48 percent. By 1933 the ranks of organized labor had shrunk to 2.5 million workers.

To look at average wages is deceptive. Buried in the 1932–33 averages were some incredibly low rates. In Detroit, the Briggs auto plant paid men 10 cents an hour and women 4 cents. In Chicago, department store salesladies earned between 5 cents and 25 cents an hour. In non-union coal fields some miners got $1.50 a day. Pennsylvania sawmills were paying 5 cents an hour. Connecticut sweatshops paid girls 60 cents to $1.10 for a 55-hour week. Farm workers averaged $1.11 a day—without board—in 1933.

Coupled with the drop in hourly pay was the drop in the number of hours and days worked. The average week for production workers went down from forty-four hours in 1929 to thirty-five in 1934, a 20 percent drop. Some workers, still listed on the payroll, got only a few days' work per month.

The steel companies were operating below 20 percent of capacity. Hundreds of thousands had been laid off and wages cut heavily. The companies claimed that they were managing to take care of their own—by relief allowances or "make work" in the mills. What this meant was reporting for turns at the mill three times a day for the chance of getting one day's work a week. The steelworker who was lucky enough to be chosen might be paid $3.60

for eight hours of work.

The black steelworker was a special victim of exploitation. In March 1930 two graduate students from Boston University studied labor conditions in the steel mills. They reported to the *New Republic:*

Plants in the South depend on the Negro for common labor, and they exploit him mercilessly. He is worked ten hours, twelve hours a day, seven days a week. White foremen—"bulldog bosses"—ride him constantly. He lives in a hovel rather than a house, and he pays the rent to the company that hires him. He is not contented, naturally, but once caught in this grinding life, poverty-stricken, ill-educated, unorganized, there is no escape for him.

One family we came to know is typical of most of the Negro steel-workers in the South. They lived in a two-room cottage—one small room serving as kitchen and dining-room the other as bedroom and parlor. There were ten children: four of them were without shoes; none had clothing decent enough to be seen in public. Their meals consisted of "white meat" and dry bread—and by "white meat" they meant pork fat, which can be bought for $.25 a pound. Once a week they have dessert with their supper. Once a year, on Christmas, they celebrate and have fruit. Amusements are out of the question; the father hardly knew what a movie was: at night he had no life in him, all he wanted was to sleep. He was working for the Thomas Steel Company, at Birmingham, getting about $3 a day for twelve hours' work.

His wages were high. The Woodward Steel Company, the Sloss and Sheffield Steel Company, and the Thomas

Steel Company, all of Birmingham, and the *Janson Steel Company* of Columbia, Pa., pay a low rate of $.24 an hour —$2.40 for a ten hour day! A few other companies—like the Tennessee Coal and Iron Company, a subsidiary of United States Steel—pay as high as $.31 an hour.

Early in the depression, labor leaders had adopted the position that "industry must work it out within itself." Counting on an early upturn in business, they supported Hoover's wage-maintenance plea. Above all, they opposed the state taking any action against unemployment. As late as October 1931, American Federation of Labor leaders pushed through a convention resolution against unemployment insurance. It was a mistake for labor, because starving unemployed men could not be prevented from strikebreaking.

In October 1931 the big textile companies of Lawrence, Massachusetts, announced a wage cut of 10 percent, and 23,000 workers walked out of the mills in protest. Their strike ended in a victory for the employers. Caught up in the fear of permanent unemployment and starvation, the workingmen voted to return to their jobs. Soon 10 percent wage cuts were being put through by the textile companies of New Bedford, Lowell, and the other milltowns.

One of the chief props of the Golden Twenties had been the automobile industry. On the eve of the crash, half a million cars were rolling off the assembly lines each month. A dash of the old spirit was still conveyed in the publicity received by the New York Automobile Show of 1931. The *Literary Digest* reported:

Merrily he rolls along, the motorist of 1931, syncro-meshing, three-speeding, four-speeding, and free-wheeling, while he hi-lees, hi-lows between low and high without stripping gears and ripping oaths. . . .

There are picturesque reports of cars so small they can slip and wriggle through the densest traffic as easily as if there were no traffic at all, of a car that has run the equivalent of two and a half times around the world in six months, to show how dependable it is, of a car that puts your eye out with its finish of tomato red and yellow.

It was a good show. But, in fact, by the end of 1929 the rate of car production had been cut back 20 percent. Production declined swiftly in steel, rubber, and other industries dependent upon automobiles.

At the onset of the depression, Henry Ford, one of auto's Big Three, had astounded everyone by announcing a seven-dollar day. This one-dollar increase over his previous daily minimum for common labor was his spectacular response to President Hoover's request that industry freeze present wages to fight off disaster. Ford's gesture was page-one news. But the publicity front of this one-man battle against the depression obscured another fact, reported by the *New York Times:* Ford was cutting wages severely in the middle and upper brackets of labor. He paid off men in one department and hired them in another at lower wages.

Ford mechanic Robert L. Cruden, who has been quoted here before, described what was actually happening inside Ford:

In the fall of that year . . . Ford stated that thenceforth $7 a day would be the minimum wage in his plants. Immediately the bosses at the Rouge plant came around saying, "Go like hell, boys. If you're gonna get that raise you gotta increase production!" On our job production was raised from fifteen pans of stock a day to twenty-two, as a result of which one entire shift of our gang was laid off. Down the line from us one man was given two drill presses to tend instead of one, as formerly. The inspector on our job was taken off and we had to do our own inspecting and still keep up the new production rate. This speed-up took place all over the plant: it is significant that, concomitant with the wage raise, nearly 30,000 men were laid off from the Rouge plant.

The claim that wages are never cut in Ford plants has always been part of the stock in trade of Ford publicity agents. But they are cut . . .

Men are "transferred" from department to department, their wages being cut as they move. I worked (in 1929) with men making $6.40 who had been making $7.20 and $7.60 before their transfer. A lathe operator of my acquaintance was recently transferred to washing, and cut from $8 to $7.60 a day. Even workers in the aristocratic Lincoln plant are not immune—last spring all those making more than a dollar an hour were cut to that figure. As a result of this process, very few workers in Ford plants now make more than $7.60 a day.

To the outsider, this may seem high wages—but most Ford workers have lately been working only three days a week. In 1930 the wages of the average Ford worker were less than a thousand dollars. Taking into account the pre-

A 1930 *luxury model Studebaker.*

President Eight Victoria, for five . . . 135-inch wheelbase . . . six wire wheels and trunk rack are standard equipment

vailing three-day week, the seven weeks of enforced idle-ness and a daily wage of $7.60, the worker made $959.20 during that year! In 1931 wages were cut and the working week reduced to one or two days a week.

Ford claims not only that there are no wage cuts in Ford plants, but there are none in any of the 3,500 plants which make parts for him . . .

The Kelsey-Hayes Wheel Company, makers of Ford wheels, has cut wages of its tool-makers from $1.10 an hour to eighty cents, and increased the hours of the night shift to fourteen a night, seven nights a week. The Detroit Gear Company, makers of small Ford parts, took a leaf out of its master's book—it laid off all men getting ninety cents an hour and rehired them at seventy-three cents. At the same time their working hours were increased from nine to eleven and a half . . .

Miners were supporting their families on as little as five dollars a week. This vivid account of a visit to a mining settlement—a company town in the West Virginia hills—was written by Edmund Wilson:

The people who work at Ward, West Virginia, live in little flat yellow houses on stilts that look like chicken-houses. They seem mean and flimsy on the sides of the hills and at the bottom of the hollow, in contrast to the magnificent mountains wooded now with the forests of mid-June. Between those round and rich-foliaged hills, through the middle of the mining settlement, runs a road which has, on one side of it, a long row of obsolete coal-cars, turned upside down and, on the other, a trickle of a creek, with bare yellow banks, half-dry yellow stones, yellowing rusty tin cans and the axles and wheels of old coal-cars. There are eight hundred or so families at Ward, two or three in most of the houses, and eight or ten children in most of the families. And these families are just as much prisoners, just as much at the mercy of the owners of their dwellings as if they did live in a chicken-yard with a high wire fence around it.

This settlement is situated in a long narrow valley which runs back among the West Virginia hills. The walls rise steep on either side, and the end of the hollow is a blind alley. The Kelley's Creek Colliery Company owns Ward, and the Paisley interests own Mammoth, another settlement further back in the hollow, where the houses are not even painted yellow and where the standard of living is lower than at Ward. The people who live in these houses mine coal from the surrounding hills. They work from eight to twelve hours a day, and they get from $2.60 to $3 for it. They are paid not in United States currency, but in chicken-feed specially coined by the companies—crude aluminum coins, thin and light and some of them with holes in the middle . . . The company "scrip" is worth, on the average, about sixty cents on the dollar. The company forces the miners to trade at the company store—the only store of course on its property—and goods are sold there at so much higher prices than at the non-company stores only three miles away that the miners never come any nearer than 60 percent to their money's worth. . . .

When times are hard, as they are at present, and the coal business, which never does well, is doing particularly badly, the operators cut their rates and make up the difference to themselves and their stockholders by getting more work for less pay out of the miners. They put in mechanical cutters and loaders, and lay off as many men as they can. According to their practice, the first to go are the men over forty-five and the men who have been crippled in the mines (at Andrew Mellon's mine, they never keep a man who has been injured). And a medical examination weeds out other classes of workmen. If it is found, for example, that you are unable to read the bottom line of type on an oculist's chart—as comparatively few people can—you are likely to be eliminated. And the result is that the children at Ward sometimes go without food for days and that they have so little to wear that they are sometimes more or less naked and cannot even be sent to the union for clothes. Even at the time when their fathers were working, they had no shoes to go to school, had hardly ever eaten fresh meat or vegetables and had never known milk since they were weaned from their mothers. Their dish consists of sow belly, potatoes and pinto beans. If they had been living in certain of the other camps, they would probably already have died from drinking water polluted by the outhouse and so escaped the pains of starvation.

From these cruel conditions came the militancy of miners during the depression years and the strikes, savagely suppressed, of West Virginia and Kentucky miners for a living wage and human dignity. This famous miner's song, which became a rallying cry for exploited workers everywhere, was composed in the spring of 1931 by Florence Reece, the wife of a coal miner living in Harlan, Kentucky:

*This company coal town in Kempton, West Virginia,
was photographed by John Vachon.*

Which Side Are You On?

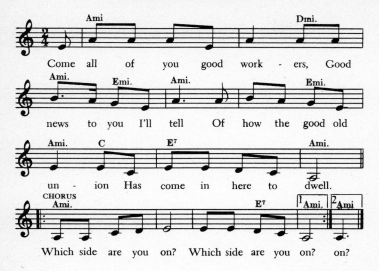

Come all of you good work - ers, Good
news to you I'll tell Of how the good old
un - ion Has come in here to dwell.

CHORUS

Which side are you on? Which side are you on? on?

My daddy was a miner,
And I'm a miner's son,
And I'll stick with the union
Till every battle's won.

CHORUS

They say in Harlan County
There are no neutrals there;
You'll either be a union man,
Or a thug for J. H. Blair.

CHORUS

Oh workers, can you stand it?
Oh tell me how you can,
Will you be a lousy scab,
Or will you be a man?

CHORUS

Don't scab for the bosses,
Don't listen to their lies,
Us poor folks haven't got a chance
Unless we organize.

CHORUS

★ 11 ★

PICKETING WITH PITCHFORKS

For America's farmers, nature added its own disaster to the man-made disaster of the depression. In the summer of 1930 came a terrible drought that dried up a belt of land all the way from Virginia on the east coast to Arkansas on the Mississippi. Ponds, streams, springs, and wells went dry, and the waters of the Mississippi sank lower than had ever been recorded. Thousands of farm families saw their cash crops wither in the fields; they had nothing left to put on their own tables.

In January 1931, reporter A. Robbins of the *Nation* toured the region to see the drought's effect. He wrote:

Even among the small farmers who own and work their own farms this has been a year of acute distress. The drought ruined their gardens, cut the corn crop in large areas to almost nothing, reduced the hay crop, and hurt their live stock. On small farm after small farm visited by the writer in several States anxious men and women were wondering how they were going to "get by." That is the general expression in the drought area. If they can just "get by" until spring; if they can just "get by" and make another crop; if it will only be a good crop year and if prices will only be a little better so they can get enough ahead by the fall of 1931 to see them through the winter of 1931–32, they will be satisfied. Gone are any thoughts of new clothes, new cars, new radios; the farmers are thinking in terms of food and feed for family and stock.

Cupboards, cellars, and closets that never before have been bare are swept clean this winter. There was little to "put up." The housewife will tell you that the garden was almost a complete failure, that the fruit did not do much, that even nuts and berries were very scarce. But the biggest worry of the average small farmer in the drought area is the problem of feed for his live stock. His cribs and barns are empty in thousands of cases. He is afraid the government feed loans will not be available in time to keep his stock from dying. In some cases the Red Cross is making allowances for feed to keep work stock alive.

Actually, for the American farmer the disaster of the 1930s was but a new depression piled on top of an old one. It had started back in 1920, after World War I. American farmers faced strong competition from the reconstructed nations of Europe. They also faced the problem caused by their own efficiency: because they could produce more than they could sell, prices dropped. It was a buyer's market, and farmers could do little to change the picture.

The farmer staggered under debts he had piled up to buy land and tools needed to meet the wartime production demands. Now he could not cut production because he hoped to earn the cash to meet the interest and the principal on his mortgage. Farm prices in the 1930s fell

The Red Cross brought some relief
to the victims of the great drought of 1930.
Here food is being distributed to
the farm families of Lonoke, Arkansas.

lower and lower, but the taxes on his land and the prices he paid for his necessities did not drop. The farmer was caught in a vise between fixed costs and falling prices.

Hoover's Federal Farm Board urged farmers to plant less so as to up their prices, but there was no incentive for doing so. From 1920 to 1932 farm production did drop 6 percent, but prices fell ten times as much—by 63 percent. Farmers could only watch in despair as corn hit 15 cents, cotton and wool 5 cents, hogs and sugar 3 cents, and beef 2.5 cents.

With farm prices so low, most farmers, living under the shadow of mortgages, knew that sooner or later they would go under. Many owners of small farms were driven into tenancy. Foreclosures and bankruptcy sales were already frequent. What was being done? Nothing that amounted to much, said Will Rogers:

I thought we was going to have some Farm Relief to report to you by this Sabbath day. But the commissions are just gathering data. They won't take the farmer's word for it that he is poor. They hire men to find out how poor he is. If they took all the money they spend on finding out how he is, and give it to the farmer he wouldn't need any more relief.

But soon as winter comes he will be O.K., soon as snow flies he can kill rabbits, that will be the biggest relief he has had so far.

There began to be reports of desperate farmers fighting to protect their families. This account is taken from *Harper's*, December 1932:

Suddenly the papers were filled with accounts of highway picketing by farmers around Sioux City. A Farmers' Holiday Association had been organized by one Milo Reno, and the farmers were to refuse to bring food to market for thirty days or "until the cost of production had been obtained."

"We have issued an ultimatum to the other groups of society," they proclaimed. "If you continue to confiscate our property and demand that we feed your stomachs and clothe your bodies we will refuse to function. We don't ask people to make implements, cloth, or houses at the price of degradation, bankruptcy, dissolution, and despair."

Reno, their first leader, was crying to them, "Agriculture as we know it has come to the parting of the ways. We will soon have no individually owned and operated farms. We have come to the place where you must practice what every other group does—strike! Or else you are not going to possess your homes."

From the Midwest, Wayne Gard reported to the *Nation* in September 1932 on the farmers' rebellion:

Torpedoes, tear gas, rotten eggs, brickbats, and planks used to puncture truck tires figure in this latest effort of our belt farmers to boost the prices of their products to the cost of production. Declaring a holiday on selling, thousands of farmers have been picketing the roads to "persuade" their neighbors to join in holding back produce for higher prices. The movement began quietly but soon was dramatized by the dumping of several truckloads of milk on a road outside Sioux City, Iowa. The pickets allowed milk and cream for hospitals to enter, however, and they donated 2,200 gallons of milk to the unemployed.

Suddenly realizing that 90 per cent of the shipments from nearby milk-producers had been cut off, Sioux City people began frantically to order milk shipped by train from Omaha and to have the blockade run by trucks bearing armed deputy sheriffs. This local milk war soon ended in a price compromise . . .

A thirty-day holiday on farm selling was begun August 8 and later was extended indefinitely. Thus far, the strike has centered mainly about the Sioux City and Omaha markets, but lately it has spread into the Dakotas, Minnesota, Wisconsin and Illinois. At the height of the Sioux City milk war, two thousand sunburned and overall-clad farmers were living in tent colonies along the nine trunk highways leading to that city. Some were armed with pitchforks for use on truck tires. But except for sporadic outbreaks the picketing has been peaceful, and truck drivers not amenable to arguments have been allowed to pass on. On August 17, a crowd of 450 farmers, equipped with clubs and brickbats, tried to remove animals from stockyard pens in Sioux City and from trucks which had run the blockade, but this attempt was repulsed by deputy sheriffs and city policemen.

Skirmishes have taken place along some of the roads. At one point outside Sioux City, pickets stopped trucks by spreading across the pavement a section of threshing-machine belt studded with menacing spikes, but this weapon was later confiscated by deputy sheriffs. In other instances, roads were blocked with railroad ties, logs, boulders, or cables. A few windshields were shattered with rocks or clubs and one sheriff was overpowered, and his gun taken from him, after he had fired a shot to warn the pickets.

Yet, in spite of such incidents, resort to force has been exceptional. The usual method of stopping trucks has been for a mass of men to stand doggedly upon the highway, in the manner of Gandhi's followers, defying the truck-drivers to crash into them. Since the drivers do not want to be guilty of manslaughter, they always stop, though some—not influenced by the arguments of the pickets—later drive on. Some of the picket forces have included women. The two rules of the patrols are "no guns and no liquor."

The picket groups have been even more active by night than by day, since much of the rural trucking is habitually done at night. Many of the picket squads have been without recognized leaders. The men come and go as they wish, but many have been on duty almost continuously.

"I'll stay till corn pickin'," one farmer declared.

"Till corn pickin'?" said another. "What do you care about corn pickin'? No use doin' all that work the way things are now."

In December of that year, 250 farmers from twenty-six states gathered in Washington for a Farmer's National Relief Conference. "Our purpose is to demand immediate action," they announced. "We are determined to stop a ruthless pressure from creditors who threaten to sweep us from our land and homes."

These were the dirt farmers themselves. What they were like and what they wanted was reported from the nation's capital by Mary Heaton Vorse, a novelist and labor journalist:

The delegates represented every known farm organization, from the radical United Farmers to the conservative Farmers' Union. Many of them of course come from their parent, the Farmers' Holiday Association. They were an impressive sight. Brown, red-faced men, broad-shouldered and strong. Some of the older men were bowed with the toil of years. Some wore working clothes, corduroy with leggings, old red and green sweaters. Blue overalls dotted the assembly, pull-over caps; other delegates wore worn and rumpled Sunday suits. It was a representative cross-section of the people who raise our foodstuffs, from whom we primarily live.

The first day was taken up with reports on conditions from every part of the country. People told how things were in their section. It was a thundering story of disaster, repeated with variations from the North to the South. It was the epic of people about to be dispossessed. It was the story in terms of individuals, of the $9,500,000,000 mortgage debt which the farmers carry, the human results of the fact that there has been a depression of ten years among the farmers. For four years the cost of production has not been made, and while the farmers make no money, their taxes in ten years have risen more than 250 per cent. Only recently in Virginia and on the same day, hundreds of farmers were evicted for the non-payment of taxes.

There were stories told of food rotting in the ground. There were stories of wool left to rot in sacks. One farmer sent a carload of sheep and was notified that the price of the sheep did not cover the cost of the freight. "I have no money," he said, "but I have more sheep." . . .

"If they come to take my farm," one farmer said, "I'm going to fight. I'd rather be killed outright than die by starvation. But before I die, I'm going to set fire to my crops, I'm going to burn my house! I'm going to p'izen my cattle!"

There was the story of the Widow Van Bohn whose husband was killed in a cyclone. Word went around her county that she was to be dispossessed. The farmers got together and went, several hundred strong, to the bankers. They assembled in great numbers the day of the sale. Thousands came from many different towns. It took three hours to clear the roads after the would-be sale. They all came to see that Widow Van Bohn kept her farm. She kept it.

There were stories of chattel-mortgage sales where all the goods were bought in for a few dollars, a quit claim was signed and a collection taken up to pay for the sale.

"In our part of the country, in Minnesota," a farmer said, "when a sale comes on, we warn people that anyone buying a place won't find life worth living there. Won't no one buy from him, sell to him—there won't nobody speak to him."

In another place where a sale was effected, only four people were allowed to bid. Telephone wires were cut to prevent people calling the sheriff . . .

I have never heard speeches which were more to the point, or which seemed the result of more mature deliberation. The farmers were generally conservative in political and social points of view; they had been driven by the relentless sweep of events into a militant position. The farmers themselves talk of this Conference as a historic occasion. They say from the platform and to each other, "We are making our Declaration of Independence as that other glorious declaration was made in Philadelphia, in 1776."

The delegates drafted a program and marched to the Capitol to present it to the Senate and the House. They asked that half a billion dollars be appropriated for immediate cash relief, with local committees of farmers to administer it. They also sought government regulation to cut the profits of food processors and other middlemen, so as to raise the prices farmers received for their crops and livestock. And they wanted no more evictions.

These proposals were read on the floors of the Senate and House, and handed to President Hoover. But Congress and the President rejected them.

Two months later farm debts were still rising. As one farm after another went on the auction block, Ferner Nuhn sent to the *Nation* in March 1933 this eyewitness account of a forced sale in Iowa:

A raw, chilly day. The yard of the farm, churned black in a previous thaw, is frozen now in ruts and nodes. Where the boots of the farmers press, a little slime of water exudes, black and shiny. Through a fence the weather-bleached stalks of corn, combed and broken by the husking, stand ghostly in the pale air. The farm buildings—machine-shed, chicken-houses, pig-houses, corncribs—sprawl and gather again in the big, hip-roofed red barn, and strike a final accent in the thrust of the tiled silo. The farm is kempt and has a going air; there is nothing run-down about it. The fields spread away, picking up other farm clusters sections off—remote, separate, dim under the big gray sky. One feels the courage of the isolate units, each swinging its big segment of earth. Perhaps they call for too much; perhaps the independence is doomed; but something of worth will be gone if it goes.

There are 300 farmers here. It is a Quaker community, long established, conservative. The farmers are mostly middle-aged, very workaday in overalls, sagging sweaters, mud-stained boots. They talk quietly in their slow, con-crete manner, move about little.

They are neighbors of a farmer who can no longer pay interest on a $2,000 mortgage. These farmers have known him for years; they know he would pay if he could. They know the debt and the interest are three times as hard to pay off now as when the mortgage was given. Some of them know that soon their own property may be endangered by defaults. They know that this particular mortgage was given on stock, and that the farmer has offered the stock in settlement. And they know that the mortgagee refused the offer, demanded a sale instead—a sale of personal property, as provided by law. . . .

The mortgagee stands off at one side, with his attorney. They are talking with the auctioneer. The farmers look that way once in a while, and while their glances are not friendly they show no open animosity. The auctioneer comes away. Some farmers surround him; they want to be reassured that no household goods will be put on sale. The auctioneer reassures them. The farmers nod grimly;

AUCTION SALE

THURSDAY, JULY 30

Sale commences at 1:00 p. m. sharp

I will sell by public auction at my farm, 10 miles west of Charlson, 31 miles northeast of Watford City, on SE quarter, Sec.9-153-96, the following personal property:

Nine Head Horses

5—Good broke work horses (2 mares, 3 geldings)
2—Saddle horses—mares
2—Mare colts, 2 years old

Five tons hay.   Four sets harness.
17 horse collars.   One saddle.

FARM MACHINERY

1—10-20 McCormick-Deering tractor
1—McCormick-Deering d.d. grain drill
——Disc harrow
1—McCormick-Deering 22-in. separator
1—Single row corn cultivator
1—Garden cultivator
5—Wagons, 2 hay racks, wagon boxes
1—Sulky plow
1—Bob sled

1—Tractor plow
1—McCormick-Deering 8-ft. binder
1—McCormick-Deering mower, good as new.
1—John Deere hay rake, new
1—Boss harrow, 5 sections
3—Gang plows
1—Ford 1-ton truck
1—Harrow cart

Other articles and equipment too numerous to mention.

TERMS--CASH.   LUNCH AT NOON

No goods to be removed from premises till settled for.

GUY WILBER, OWNER

M. S. STENEHJEM, Auctioneer   First International Bank, Clerk.

*Farmers who failed saw everything
they owned go on the auction block.*

that much has been accomplished anyway. There are no leaders, no haranguers, no organization. In fact, this is the first affair of the sort in the county.

There is a movement toward the barns. The auctioneer mounts a wagon. The first thing offered is a mare. It is rather strange that live stock is offered first; the usual order is machinery first. The defaulting farmer stands silent holding the mare; he is a man almost elderly, quiet, staid-appearing; and he stands embarrassed, smoothing the mane of the mare. The auctioneer goes through his regular cry. The mare is sixteen years old, sound except for a wire cut and a blue eye. What is he offered, what is he offered, what is he offered, does he hear a bid? He tries to make it sound like an ordinary sale. But the crowd stands silent, grim. At last someone speaks out. Two dollars. Two dollars! Unheard of, unbelievable, why she's worth twenty times that!

The silence of the farmers is like a thick wall. The rigmarole of the auctioneer beats against it, and falls back in his face. The farmer holding the mare stands with his head hanging. At last, without raising his eyes, he says, "Fifteen dollars." This is a new and distressing business to him, and he is ashamed to make a bid of less than that.

". . . do I hear a twenty, a twenty, a twenty? Why she's worth twice that much." The auctioneer is still going through the make-believe. He keeps it up for five more minutes. A pause, and a voice speaks out, "Sell her." It is not loud, but there is insistence in it, like the slice of a plow, with the tractor-pull of the crowd reinforcing it. The auctioneer hesitates, gives in. The silent, waiting crowd is too much. "Sold." After that there is less make-believe.

Three more horses are offered. They are knocked down to the farmer, with no other bids, for ten dollars, eight dollars, a dollar and a half. The farmer is learning. The machinery comes next. A hay rack, a wagon, two plows, a binder, rake, mower, disc-harrow, cultivator, pulverizer. A dollar, fifty cents, fifty cents, a quarter, a half a dollar. Sold to the farmer. His means of livelihood are saved to him.

But the tax and mortgage sales went on. Between 1930 and 1935 about 750,000 farms were lost through foreclosure and bankruptcy sales.

★ 12 ★

TROUBLE COMES, TROUBLE GOES

Almost half the nation's farmers during these years were tenants who did not own their own land or tools. Every month the crisis forced thousands of small owners, unable to meet their mortgage payments, from independence into tenancy. They were near the bottom of the farm ladder, and with them were black and white sharecroppers.

Now, throughout the cotton and tobacco regions of the South, as cotton sank to prices not seen for thirty years—five cents a pound—thousands of tenants, sharecroppers, and farm laborers voiced their misery. Here is one of their songs, "Hard Times Blues":

Well, I went down home 'bout a year ago
Things so bad, Lord, my heart was sore
Folks had nothin', it was a sin and a shame
Ev'rybody said hard times was to blame.

CHORUS:
Great God a-mighty, folks feelin' bad
Lost ev'rything they ever had.

Now the sun was a-shinin' fourteen days and no rain
Hoeing and planting was all in vain

They had hard, hard times, Lord, all around
Meal barrels empty, crops burnt to the ground

CHORUS

They had skinny lookin' children, bellies poking out
That old pellagry without a doubt
Old folks hangin' 'round the cabin door
Ain't seen times so hard before.

CHORUS

Well, I went to the boss at the commissary store
Folks all starvin', please don't close your door
We want more food and a little more time to pay
Boss man laughed and walked away.

CHORUS

Now your landlord comes around when your rent it is
  due
And if you ain't got his money he'll take your home
  from you
He'll take your mule and horse, even take your cow
Get off my land, you're no good no how.

CHORUS

Farm tenancy dated prior to the Civil War. Sharecropping was a remnant of the plantation system which never effectively broke up. The planter was still lord of the manor. Instead of slave labor, black freedmen and poor whites served as sharecroppers or tenant farmers. The sharecropper exchanged his and his family's labor for a share of the crop he raised. To buy his food and clothing, he borrowed at high interest rates from the landlord and paid town merchants credit charges that might run up to

50 percent. Often cheated and lied to, kept illiterate, ragged, hungry, he and the stock and the land grew poorer year by year.

For black sharecroppers, hopelessness was in the song they hummed as they hacked the earth with their hoes:

> *Trouble comes, trouble goes,*
> *I done had my share of woes.*
> *Times get better by 'n' by.*
> *But then my time will come to die.*

Year after year of the cycle led only to despair. "Ain't make nothing, don't speck nothing no more till I die. Eleven bales of cotton and the man take it all. We jest work for de other man. He git everything."

From a special field study made at that time by two Smith College economists, Katharine DuPre Lumpkin and Dorothy Wolff Douglas, comes this account of a boy growing up in a black sharecropper's family:

> *Tom is a sharecropper's child, black, in Alabama. His family (father, mother, and four children old enough to make "hands") all work for the landowner, are all collectively and continually in debt to him (they get $75 worth of supplies for the growing season and he keeps the books), and all live in a two-room cabin . . .*
>
> *Tom is now twelve and old enough to be counted by the Census. (The Census enumeration begins at age ten.) But even six years ago in the year of the last Census, Tom was at work, though officially nonexistent, along with the thousands of his little fellow laborers, at age six, beginning to pick cotton.*

Tom gets up, or is pulled out of bed, at four o'clock in summer, by his older brother, who is quicker than he to hear the landlord's bell. Work for the entire plantation force is "from can see to can't see" (i.e., from daylight to dark), and the bell is their commanding timepiece. . . .

Tom is a good, steady chopper and can do over half a man's work. At picking he can do two-thirds. Peter, aged nine, does considerably less than that. In fact when his father asked to stay on at the beginning of the growing season, the landlord told him he didn't see how he could keep him on another year raising a crop on so many acres and living in such a good house, with his family so "no-account."

Tom has been to school part of three grades. The Negro school in his district runs four months "normally" (the white school runs six); but in the year 1932–33 it closed altogether, and since then it has been averaging less than three months. Besides, cotton-picking season in Alabama runs well into November, and after that it is often too cold to go to school without shoes. So from January on Tom and Peter have been taking turns in one pair . . .

In picking cotton Tom is not so much "smarter" than some of the younger children. At age twelve he can keep going longer, of course, at the end of a twelve-hour day with the thermometer still close to 100 degrees, than he could when he was seven, but he can hardly pick faster. All the children pick with both hands, and by the end of the first season the lifetime rhythm of pluck, pluck, drop-in-the-bag is long since established. But now that Tom is taller he has to stoop so much, or move along on his knees, while the littlest fellows scramble by with "hardly a bend

*At thirteen, long out of school, this young
sharecropper living near Americus, Georgia,
was working in the fields from
"can see" to "can't see."*

to them." The cotton plants often grow shoulder-high, to be sure, but the cotton bolls on them grow nearly all the way to the ground; so, for all but a tiny child, this means "stooping, stooping all day." But Tom can manage the big sack that he drags after him by a shoulder strap better now than when he was a little fellow. It grows so heavy dragging along after the smallest pickers all day that it nearly makes up for the "bends" of the older ones.

Chopping cotton is much harder and is done under greater pressure for time, for the growing season will not wait. The six- and seven-year-old children do not engage in this, but Tom has long since become experienced. He handles the heavy hoe with a ready swing, cutting out the superfluous plants with a steady chop, chop, chop, from sunrise to dark.

It was almost impossible for black croppers in the South to rebel against a life like Tom's. In the summer of 1931 black sharecroppers near Camp Hill, Alabama, tried to form a union. When they met in a church, the sheriff's posse raided it, burned it to the ground, and fired on the fleeing croppers. One Negro was killed, three wounded, and seventeen arrested, of whom four mysteriously disappeared.

Throughout the Thirties, dispossessed croppers and tenants whose leases had not been renewed took to the road, joining the nation's harvest hands and migrant workers. They followed the seasonal crops as pickers and laborers, and earned an average of $110 in 1933. This research monograph, recorded by John N. Webb, pictures twelve months in a migrant worker's life:

July-October 1932. Picked figs at Fresno, Calif., and vicinity. Wages, 10 cents a box, average 50-pound box. Picked about 15 boxes a day to earn $1.50; about $40 a month.

October-December 1932. Cut Malaga and muscat (table and wine) grapes near Fresno. Wages, 25 cents an hour. Average 6-hour day, earning $1.50; about $40 a month.

December 1932. Left for Imperial Valley, Calif.

February 1933. Picked peas, Imperial Valley. Wages, 1 cent a pound. Average 125 pounds a day. Earned $30 for season. Also worked as wagon-man in lettuce field on contract. Contract price, 5 cents a crate repack out of packing house; not field pack. This work paid 60 cents to $1 a day. On account of weather, was fortunate to break even at finish of season. Was paying 50 cents a day room and board.

March-April 1933. Left for Chicago. Stayed a couple of weeks. Returned to California two months later.

May 1933. Odd-jobs on lawns, radios, and victrolas at Fresno. Also worked as porter and handy man.

June 1933. Returned to picking figs near Fresno. Wages, 10 cents a box. Averaged $1.50 a day, and earned $50 in two months.

The seasonal pickers and migrant workers often lived in camps of tents or dilapidated shacks. Reporter John L. Spivak wrote of his visit to one in an agricultural valley of California:

Just take the main highway from Fresno, Calif., to Mendota which is about thirty miles away and turn west at Mendota for about four miles. You can't miss it because you'll see a big sign "Land of Milk and Honey." When you've passed this sign you'll see against the horizon a cluster of houses and when you come to the sign "Hotchkiss Ranch—Cotton Pickers Wanted" turn up the side road a few hundred yards beyond the comfortable farm house with its barns and cotton shelters. There's a row of fifteen outhouses along the road. . . .

There are two more outhouses a little way from these and those are the ones actually used for outhouses. You can tell that by the odor and the swarms of flies that hover around these two especially. This is a typical migratory workers' camp, only some have five outhouses for the workers and some have thirty. It depends upon the size of the farm. . . .

In this outhouse where a baby girl has scarlet fever you'll find an iron bedstead. That's where the baby sleeps, the one that's tossing around in fever while the mother tries to shoo the flies away. That's the only bed and it's one of the five in the whole camp, so you can't miss it. The other six in this family sleep on the floor huddled together; father, mother, two grown brothers, a little brother, and the fifteen-year-old girl. They sleep like most everyone else in the camp: on the floor.

That barrel and rusty milk can in the corner of the room where everybody sleeps on the floor holds the water they bring from Mendota to cool the child's fever. It is four miles to Mendota and four miles back and eight miles costs a little for gas so they have to be very sparing with the water. That's why they all look so dirty—it's not because they don't like to wash. It's because it costs too much to get water—water needed for cooking and drinking. You can't waste water just washing yourself when it costs so much to get. After all, when you make thirty-five cents for a full day's work and spend some of that for gas to get water it leaves you that much less for food. . . .

When I walked out in the field there was this little girl dragging a huge sack along the furrow, and stuffing the brown bolls into it. She looked so tired, so weary and then I noticed that she was with child.

"How old are you?" I asked.

She looked up and smiled pleasantly. "Fifteen."

"Working in the fields long?"

"Uh-uh."

"How old were you when you started?"

She shrugged shoulders. "Dunno. Maybe eight. Maybe nine. I dunno."

"What do you make a day?"

"Sometimes in first picking dollar and a half. We get seventy-five cents a hundred. Used to get sixty cents but red agitators got us fifteen cents raise. But for third picking get only forty cents a hundred and there ain't so much to pick."

By age sixteen folksinger Woody Guthrie was roving his "big green universe" to take work where he could find it. He said of those times, as the drought worsened in the mid-Thirties:

There's a whole big army of us rambling workers—call us migrants. Hundreds of thousands of people fighting

A dispossessed Arkansas farm family
on the road in search of work.
The photograph is by Ben Shahn.

against all kinds of odds to keep their little families sticking together; trickling along the highways and railroad tracks; living in dirty little shack towns, hunkered down along the malaria creeks, squatting in the wind of the dust-blown plains, and stranded like wild herds of cattle across the blistered deserts.

A whole army of us. It's a big country. But we can take it. We can sing you songs so full of hard traveling, and hard sweating and hard fighting you'll get big clear blisters in the palms of your hands just listening to us.

Singing and playing his harmonica or guitar, he wrote many songs about the migrants. One was "Pastures of Plenty":

Pastures of Plenty

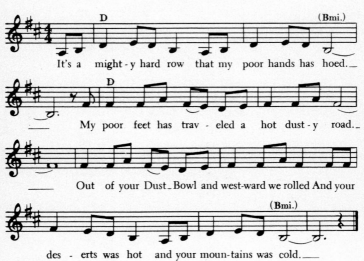

It's a might-y hard row that my poor hands has hoed.

My poor feet has trav-eled a hot dust-y road.

Out of your Dust Bowl and west-ward we rolled And your des-erts was hot and your moun-tains was cold.

I worked in your orchards of peaches and prunes,
I slept on the ground in the light of the moon;
On the edge of the city you'll see us and then,
We come with the dust and we go with the wind.

California, Arizona, I make all your crops,
Well, it's up north up to Oregon to gather your hops;
Dig the beets from your ground, cut the grapes from your vine,
To set on your table your light, sparkling wine.

It's always we rambled, that river and I,
All along your green valley I will work till I die;
My land I'll defend with my life if it be,
'Cause my pastures of plenty must always be free.

★ 13 ★

WHICH WAY?

Which way would the millions, in their anguish and frustration after three years of the depression, turn? Would they follow some rightist rabble-rouser, or move left along the route marked out by Soviet Russia? Their faith in the virtues of private enterprise had been badly shaken by the crisis.

The first sign of protest came only four months after Black Thursday on Wall Street. On March 6, 1930, Communists organized demonstrations in many major cities. WORK OR WAGES! DON'T STARVE—FIGHT! were the slogans on their banners and placards. About a million unemployed marched in the streets for relief and unemployment insurance. At New York City's Union Square, police charged the 35,000 demonstrators with clubs. The New York World reported that women were "struck in the face with blackjacks, boys beaten by gangs of seven and eight policemen, and an old man backed into a doorway and knocked down time after time, only to be dragged to his feet and struck with fist and club."

Cleveland saw a bloody riot of 10,000 that day. In Philadelphia, Chicago, Los Angeles, Seattle, the unemployed marched on city halls. Often Communist organizers had a hand in the demonstrations, for few others were doing anything. Small as the radical party was—fewer than 10,000 members, most of them new—it led the way in calling for government relief, work projects, and unemployment insurance.

Soon there were councils, leagues, and alliances to direct the unemployed in their growing protest movement. Some were led by Communists, others by Socialists or independent radicals. Violence there was, but the disorders were local and sporadic. From the *New York Herald Tribune*:

England, Arkansas, Jan. 3, 1931. The long drought that ruined hundreds of Arkansas farms last summer had a dramatic sequel late today when 500 farmers, most of them white men and many of them armed, marched on the business section of this town. . . . Shouting that they must have food for themselves and their families, the invaders announced their intention to take it from the stores unless it were provided from some other source without cost.

From the *New York Times*:

Oklahoma City, Jan. 20, 1931. A crowd of men and women, shouting that they were hungry and jobless, raided a grocery store near the City Hall today. Twenty-six of the men were arrested.

From United Press:

Detroit, July 9, 1931. An incipient riot by 500 unemployed men turned out of the city lodging house for lack of funds was quelled by police reserves in Cadillac Square tonight.

From Federated Press:

Indiana Harbor, Indiana, Aug. 15, 1931. Fifteen hundred jobless men stormed the plant of the Fruit Growers Express Company here, demanding that they be given jobs to keep from starving. The company's answer was to call the city police, who routed the jobless with menacing clubs.

The marches for jobless benefits culminated in a National Unemployment Insurance Day on February 4, 1932. Despite heavy rains and blizzards, crowds demonstrated in over 100 towns and cities to protest the failure of government and business to do anything against starvation. As before, there were arrests, but what was new was that the movement had now spread into the smaller places, even to the South and Far West.

Most important were signs that the employed were beginning to understand that unemployment benefits were as necessary to them as to the jobless. The rank-and-file union membership now faced their leaders—who had said earlier that "industry must work it out within itself" —with strong opposition. The lower middle class, too— small shopkeepers, small landlords—began to see that unemployment insurance would indirectly benefit them. The jobless simply did not buy, nor could they pay rent. Federal benefits would pass from them to shopkeepers and landlords.

Many professionals, artists especially, were drawn into the heart of the economic storm. Photographers such as Dorothea Lange, Walker Evans, Margaret Bourke-White, and John Vachon documented drought and flood, share-

*Unemployed Chicagoans demonstrating
for work relief at the corner of Monroe and
Sangamon Streets in February, 1932.*

cropper and migrant, breadline and Hooverville. Writers shaped into words images of depression-torn America. John Dos Passos, Edmund Wilson, Malcolm Cowley, Erskine Caldwell, James Agee, John Steinbeck, Langston Hughes, Sherwood Anderson were turning to social reporting. Delegations of students, clergymen, and writers visited the minefields of Kentucky and southern Illinois. The most publicized expedition was that led by novelist Theodore Dreiser to Harlan County, Kentucky, in 1931 to investigate reports of violence against the miners.

Perhaps the most dramatic protest of the period was the Bonus Army march on Washington in the spring of 1932. Veterans of World War I, starting with only 300 from Oregon and gathering strength as they moved, came to lobby in Congress for passage of the Patman Bill. The Bill proposed immediate payment of a veteran's bonus, authorized by Congress in 1924, but not due and payable until 1945. Over a quarter of a million ex-soldiers, jobless and hungry, needed that money now, but President Hoover opposed paying them. Nevertheless, Congress had paid them about half the bonus over his veto. Now 20,000 veterans were demanding the other half.

From Washington, John Dos Passos reported on the camp the Bonus Army had pitched on the edge of the nation's capital:

Now they are camped on Anacostia Flats in the southeast corner of Washington. Nearly twenty thousand of them altogether. Everywhere you meet new ragged troups straggling in. A few have gone home discouraged, but very few. Anacostia Flats is the recruiting center; from there they are sent to new camps scattered around the out-skirts of Washington. Anacostia Flats is the ghost of an army camp from the days of the big parade, with its bugle calls, its messlines, greasy K.P.'s, M.P.'s, headquarters, liaison officers, medical officer. Instead of the tents and the long tarpaper barracks of those days, the men are sleeping in little leantos built out of old newspapers, cardboard boxes, packing crates, bits of tin or tarpaper roofing, old shutters, every kind of cockeyed makeshift shelter from the rain scraped together out of the city dump.

The doughboys have changed too, as well as their uni-forms and their housing, in these fifteen years. There's the same goulash of faces and dialects, foreigners' pidgin Eng-lish, lingoes from industrial towns and farming towns, East, Northeast, Middle West, Southwest, South, but we were all youngsters then; now we are getting on into middle life, sunken eyes, hollow cheeks off breadlines, palelooking knotted hands of men who've worked hard with them, and then for a long time have not worked. In these men's faces, as in Pharaoh's dream, the lean years have eaten up the fat years already. . . .

In the middle of the Anacostia camp is a big platform with a wooden object sticking up from one corner that looks like an old-fashioned gallows. Speaking goes on from this platform all morning and all afternoon. The day I saw it, there were a couple of members of the bonus army's congressional committee on the platform, a Negro in an overseas cap and a tall red Indian in buckskin and beads, wearing a tengallon hat. The audience, white men and Negroes, is packed in among the tents and shelters. A tall scrawny man with deeply sunken cheeks is talking.

He's trying to talk about the bonus but he can't stick to it, before he knows it he's talking about the general economic conditions of the country:

"Here's a plant that can turn out everything every man, woman, and child in this country needs, from potatoes to washing machines, and it's broken down because it can't give the fellow who does the work enough money to buy what he needs with. Give us the money and we'll buy their bread and their corn and beans and their electric iceboxes and their washing machines and their radios. We ain't holding out on 'em because we don't want those things. Can't get a job to make enough money to buy 'em, that's all."

In mid-June the Senate overwhelmingly rejected the Patman Bill. Early in July, to get the demonstrators out of sight, Congress voted to pay their passage home. About 5,000 left Washington and their makeshift camp. With Congress adjourned, rumors floated about that the Hoover Administration was ready to oust the remaining bonus seekers, by force if necessary. It was hard to believe. The President was already campaigning for re-election, on the platform that his wisdom had kept the country peaceful and the unemployed quiet and loyal. Would he be foolish enough to use bayonets against war veterans bearing petitions?

Paul Y. Anderson reported for the *Nation* the choice the President made:

Hoover's campaign for re-election was launched Thursday, July 28, at Pennsylvania Avenue and Third Street, with four troops of cavalry, four companies of infantry, a mounted machine-gun squadron, six whippet tanks, 300 city policemen and a squad of Secret Service men and Treasury agents. Among the results immediately achieved were the following:

Two veterans of the World War shot to death; one eleven-week-old baby in a grave condition from gas, shock, and exposure; one eight-year-old boy partially blinded by gas; two policemen's skulls fractured; one by-stander shot through the shoulder; one veteran's ear severed with a cavalry saber; one veteran stabbed in the hip with a bayonet; more than a dozen veterans, police-men, and soldiers injured by bricks and clubs; upward of 1,000 men, women, and children gassed, including police-men, reporters, ambulance drivers, and residents of Wash-ington; and approximately $10,000 worth of property destroyed by fire, including clothing, food, and temporary shelters of the veterans and a large amount of building material owned by a government contractor.

Anderson and other reporters said they believed the troops, commanded by General Douglas MacArthur, were used to evict the veterans from Washington for a political purpose, "to persuade the American people that their government was threatened with actual overthrow, and that the courage and decisiveness of Herbert Hoover had averted revolution." Tanks, gas, sabers, bayonets, and fire had been used against unarmed men, women, and chil-dren "to show the country that the danger of 'insurrection' was real and that the Administration had prepared to meet it," wrote Anderson.

As the gassed and wounded veterans fled Washington,

*The veterans of the Bonus Army fought off
the troops with any weapon at hand.*

Malcolm Cowley of the *New Republic* followed them. In Pennsylvania he caught up with them at a temporary camp and talked to some of the Bonus Marchers:

Mile after mile we passed the ragged line as we too drove northward to the camp at Ideal Park. We were carrying two of the veterans, chosen from a group of three hundred by a quick informal vote of their comrades. One was a man gassed in the Argonne and tear-gassed at Anacostia; he breathed with an effort, as if each breath would be his last. The other was a man with family troubles; he had lost his wife and six children during the retreat from Camp Marks and hoped to find them in Johnstown. He talked about his service in France, his three medals, which he refused to wear, his wounds, his five years in a government hospital. "If they gave me a job," he said, "I wouldn't care about the bonus. . . . Now I don't ever want to see a flag again. Give me a gun and I'll go back to Washington." — "That's right, buddy," said a woman looking up from her two babies, who lay on a dirty quilt in the sun. A cloud of flies hovered above them. Another man was reading the editorial page of a Johnstown paper. He shouted, "Let them come here and mow us down with machine guns. We won't move this time." — "That's right, buddy," said the woman again. A haggard face—eyes bloodshot, skin pasty white under a three days' beard— suddenly appeared at the window of the car. "Hoover must die," said the face ominously. "You know what this means?" a man shouted from the other side. "This means revolution." — "Yes, you're damned right it means revolution."

The Bonus Army straggled
out of the capital and headed—
where? Homeward?
Many no longer had a home.

But it didn't. Bread riots and hunger marches "do not necessarily mean revolution," as economist George Soule wrote in *Harper's* that August. "People may smash windows because they are hungry without wanting a governmental overturn or knowing how to bring it about."

It was ordinary folk who made up the Bonus Army, just as they made up the millions of unemployed. They were farm workers and factory hands, skilled mechanics and white-collar workers, foremen and professionals. "Every one of them has been thoroughly whipped by his individual economic circumstances," said Mauritz Hallgren. "There is about the lot of them an atmosphere of hopelessness, of utter despair, though not of desperation. They have no enthusiasm whatever, and no stomach for fighting."

Many of their feelings—patriotism, but protest and disillusionment too—were expressed in the song "Brother, Can You Spare a Dime?" It spoke for the man who had a dream and who had worked hard to fulfill it, only to find himself outside and forgotten. Its poignant music is still heard today, for the song lives in the American memory:

Brother, Can You Spare A Dime?

They used to tell me I was building a dream,
And so I followed the mob—
When there was earth to plough or guns to bear
I was always there—right there on the job.
They used to tell me I was building a dream
With peace and glory ahead—
Why should I be standing in line
Just waiting for bread?

Once I built a railroad, made it run,
Made it race against time.
Once I built a railroad,
Now it's done—
Brother, can you spare a dime?
Once I built a tower, to the sun.
Brick and rivet and lime,
Once I built a tower,
Now it's done—
Brother, can you spare a dime?
Once in khaki suits,
Gee, we looked swell,
Full of that Yankee Doodle-de-dum.
Half a million boots went sloggin' thru Hell,
I was the kid with the drum.
Say don't you remember, they called me Al—
It was Al all the time.
Say, don't you remember I'm your pal—
Buddy, can you spare a dime?

No, America was not moving toward revolution. Some editors, bankers, industrialists, generals, and politicians feared revolution was around the corner, and many radicals hoped or believed it was. Changes were coming, and very soon, but they would be evolutionary. Political power would move from one party to another, not from one class to another. But the changes would make a great difference in the lives of the dispossessed.

★ |14| ★

FORGING NEW TOOLS

In April 1932, Kansas editor William Allen White wrote a letter to a friend, Walter Lippman, the political columnist. Both men were Republicans, and both were deeply shaken by the depression. In his letter, White said:

If out of this thing cannot come some permanent peace of mind and economic security for the average man, the manual laborer, the small fellow who has other talents than the acquisitive faculties, we will have lost the world as well as our own souls. If the fear motive is to persist on and on as the prod in the pants of humanity, if we cannot supplant hope and joy for fear, if the capacity for financial reward is to be the sum of all our virtues, what's the use of all this travail?

Travelers crossing America that summer saw a land of harsh contrasts. Surplus food was being spilled into the ocean or piled high in grain elevators while men were breaking store windows to steal a loaf of bread. Shoe factories were shut down in New England while children stayed home from school because they had nothing to put on their feet. Billions of dollars nestled safely in bank vaults while hundreds of cities issued scrip because they had no currency to pay their bills. Families went in ragged clothing while farmers could not market millions of bales of cotton. All this in the richest country on earth, with the fattest acres, the tallest buildings, the mightiest machinery, the biggest factories.

Who was to blame?

Some business leaders placed the blame on the victims. John Edgerton, President of the National Association of Manufacturers, said that if the jobless "do not practice the habits of thrift and conservation, or if they gamble away their savings on the stock market or elsewhere, is our economic system, or government, or industry to blame?"

After three years of the depression, there were only a few who thought that way. The country was bitter at the spectacle of want amid plenty. It was drifting on a sea of doubt, uncertain where to turn, what the answers might be.

In the summer of 1932 the Republicans renominated Herbert Hoover for the presidency. They did it hopelessly: to do otherwise would have been to indict their own leadership. The man in the stiff, high collar who had preached "rugged individualism" was now identified with "ragged individualism." The make-it-on-your-own philosophy that had elevated him from Iowa farm boy to multimillionaire had failed too many of his countrymen. Campaigning in the West, Hoover could feel the people's hatred for him. He became a universal target for bitter jokes. One said that of course he was the world's greatest engineer: "In a little more than two years he has drained, ditched, and damned the United States."

By the grim winter of 1932–33 the word "depression" seemed to have a permanent sound to it. A sense of hopelessness gripped the nation. America was finished. Some looked for a dictator; others talked of a supercouncil of business leaders. The financial weekly *Barron's* said:

Of course we all realize that dictatorships and semidictatorships in peace time are all quite contrary to the spirit of American institutions and all that. And yet— well, a genial and light-hearted dictator might be a relief.

The Democrats nominated a man as hopeful as Hoover was discouraged—Franklin Delano Roosevelt of New York. They were sure to win, no matter who their candidate was, so long as his name was not Hoover. But FDR was also a great campaigner. He had been a state senator, Assistant Secretary of the Navy under Wilson, and vice-presidential candidate in 1920. When polio cut him down, with quiet courage he learned to live with a permanently crippled body and re-entered politics, winning the governorship of New York in 1928. In his four years in office he had shown concern for the unemployed. He had been the first governor to set up a state relief agency. During his vigorous, confident presidential campaign he talked about "the forgotten man at the bottom of the economic pyramid."

The grin, the battered old felt hat, the jauntily clenched cigarette holder were a happy contrast to his dour opponent. The tragic illness he had endured and surmounted made many feel that, rich though he was, he could understand the suffering and poverty of those who struggled to make a living. Although his platform was strikingly similar to Hoover's, FDR promised experimentation and change. He carried all but six states, getting 22 million votes against Hoover's 15 million.

A sign of how cold people were to communism came in the vote for that party's candidate, William Z. Foster. He got 100,000 votes. Socialist Norman Thomas did better, with 900,000 votes, but his party won proportionately far less votes than in 1920 or 1912.

In the worst years some thought that America had no choice before it but socialism or ruin. Most Americans did not think that way. They were pragmatists, that is, they dealt with a problem when it came up. If the thing they tried didn't work, they wrestled with it again and came up with another answer. If something fails, try something else. That was how Americans looked at their problems, no matter how big or small. Few envisioned a single solution that would solve all problems. Not many believed such an answer was possible or that it would not do more harm than good.

The promise of America was more than hard work, thrift, and individual enterprise could bring about. These years had proved that. The crisis had been too deep, too terrible, too enduring to leave things as they were. But although no panaceas were produced that caught the imagination or faith of the majority, many began to think that both business and government needed to develop a social conscience. Both should be made to work for the benefit of man. They knew the goal of business was profits and that the government, up to this time, never wished to interfere with that goal, no matter what the social cost. But three years of the depression had been lesson enough for the unemployed. And for the many others more fortunate who could not stand by and see such suffering without desiring some kind of action to end it, or at least ease it.

"Business was business," of course. Certainly the depression was no one man's fault. But if business as a system had no social sense, people felt it was time that government—if it was truly the representative of all the people—stepped in and prevented business from making the mistakes that led to the Great Depression.

Roosevelt, while offering nothing definite in his campaign, promised a "New Deal." The times were on the side of anyone who promised to act, to move, to do *something, anything.*

On Inauguration Day—March 4, 1933—the country was the nearest it had ever been to complete breakdown. The Saturday sky was chill and cloudy. The crowd packed in front of the Capitol shivered in the raw air as it watched Hoover, walking alone, take his seat on the platform. Then Roosevelt appeared, supported by his son James. The Chief Justice gave the oath of office, and in a clear, strong voice the new President told his audience: "The only thing we have to fear is fear itself."

Roosevelt acted, and swiftly. He asked for and used broad executive powers to wage war against the emergency. Called into special session, Congress in 100 days passed bill after bill, many of them half thought out or

*President Roosevelt with Governor and Mrs. Gifford Pinchot
at the Decoration Day ceremonies at Gettysburg in 1934.*

experimental, but aimed at bringing about economic recovery. Federal relief came first, and then billions to provide public works so the unemployed could find jobs at last.

By November of 1933, 4 million people were back at work. Farmers were helped with crop-control programs that raised farm prices, and their mortgage burden was lifted. "Economic planning" was the new phrase on every tongue. It was not at all a socialist blueprint, but a patchwork of plans improvised for the hour by the lawyers, economists, and sociologists whom the New Deal brought into government service. Their function was to save capitalism, a goal Roosevelt declared publicly. In the next few years controls were devised to regulate business and finance, and to limit the likelihood of a giddy swing like the Twenties. Labor was helped by a law that protected its right to organize; by unemployment insurance, social security, low-cost housing, and wage-and-hour laws. Still, for reasons this book has not room for, unemployment persisted through the 1930s. It is cause for thought that it took the menace of Hitler and the war crisis of 1939 to put every employable American to work again in the booming defense industries.

That year President Roosevelt looked back on the depression and the changes it had wrought in America's thinking. At the Jackson Day dinner he said:

Today there is emerging a real and forceful belief on the part of the great mass of the people that honest, intelligent and courageous government can solve many problems which the average individual cannot face alone in a world where there are no longer one hundred and twenty acres of good free land for everybody.

Speaking to Congress the same year, he added:

The tools of government which we had in 1933 are outmoded. We have had to forge new tools for a new role of government in a democracy—a role of new responsibility for new needs and increased responsibility for old needs, long neglected.

Thirty years and at least two wars later, in the richest country on earth, close to 50 million Americans still live below the level of human decency. They go without adequate food, housing, medical care, and education. They make up "the other America," the poor America that affluent America has for too long been blind to.

The problems of the poor have not yet been solved. The welfare state born out of the suffering of the Great Depression has not reached those who need its help most. These poor—the migrant workers, the unskilled, the old, the minorities—have gone on living in black ghettos and Appalachian valleys, in rural slums, in rooming houses and ill-maintained nursing homes. They are, in social critic Michael Harrington's words, "the victims of the very inventions and machines that have provided a higher standard of living for the rest of the society. They are upside-down in the economy, and for them greater productivity often means worse jobs; agricultural advance becomes hunger."

In the spring of 1968 the Citizens Board of Inquiry into Hunger and Malnutrition found that over 10 million

*In the spring of 1968 the Poor People's March came
to Washington and, like the Bonus Marchers 36 years earlier,
pitched camp in what was soon called Resurrection City.
Congressional indifference or hostility buried their hopes, and
they finally left with little promised or accomplished.*

Americans are suffering from hunger and that 20 million more do not get a proper diet. In the same month, *Fortune* magazine published its annual survey of the richest Americans. It reported two (J. Paul Getty and Howard Hughes) worth over $1 billion, six worth at least $500 million, and 153 worth over $100 million.

Earlier in this book the gap between the richest and the poorest in the 1920s was discussed as a factor in bringing about the depression. The gap is still there—and it is a dangerous social fact. The resources of our country are rich enough to rescue the generations of poor the Great Depression left behind. A war on poverty is not a new idea. But revolts in the ghettos and marches on Washington show that it has not yet been waged with the will and the daring simple justice demands.

BIBLIOGRAPHY

This bibliography includes many of the sources used in preparing this book and offers suggestions for further reading. An asterisk* marks those books available in paperback, and most are currently in print.

Books

A fine and very readable GENERAL narrative, full of the details of everyday life during a prolonged crisis and lightened by anecdotes is *Caroline Bird, *The Invisible Scar*, New York: Pocket Books, 1967. Also highly recommended is *David A. Shannon, ed., *The Great Depression*, Englewood Cliffs: Prentice Hall, 1960. It has 56 documentary accounts grouped by topic, including farmers, nomads, relief education, bank failures, and case histories. *Arthur M. Schlesinger, Jr., *The Crisis of the Old Order 1919–1933* (*The Age of Roosevelt*, vol. 1), Boston: Houghton Mifflin, 1957, is a richly detailed and beautifully written history of the pre-FDR era. It gives vivid portraits of many leading figures, and includes a biography of Franklin Roosevelt. An excellent social history (no longer in print) is Dixon Wecter, *The Age of the Great Depression 1929–1941*, New York: The Macmillan Company, 1948.

For ECONOMICS, there is Broadus Mitchell, *Depression Decade: From New Era Through New Deal 1929–1941*, New

York: Holt, Rinehart and Winston, 1947; and *John Kenneth Galbraith, *The Great Crash 1929*, Boston: Houghton Mifflin, 1955. The latter lays bare the anatomy of the financial disaster in a crisp and witty style. A chapter on the big brokerage houses such as Goldman Sachs will be particularly helpful.

For CONTEMPORARY ACCOUNTS, perhaps the most moving is Mauritz A. Hallgren, *Seeds of Revolt*, New York: Alfred A. Knopf, 1933 (out of print). Hallgren, an associate editor of the *Nation* then, was a brilliant observer, sympathetic and yet objective in evaluating the significance of what he saw. His theme is the protest movement including the auto strikes in Detroit and the plight of the coal miners in Harlan, Kentucky. Another superb period book, from which I have quoted on coal miners in West Virginia, is *Edmund Wilson, *The American Earthquake*, Garden City, N.Y.: Doubleday and Company (Anchor), 1968. It contains the author's magazine articles written during the Twenties and Thirties.

There are several good LITERARY ANTHOLOGIES of the era. In *Louis Filler, ed., *The Anxious Years: America in the 1930's*, New York: G. P. Putnam's Sons (Capricorn), 1964, selections represent the writings of Sherwood Anderson, William Saroyan, Erskine Caldwell, Edward Dahlberg, S. J. Perelman, and others. *Harvey Swados, ed., *The American Writer and the Great Depression*, Indianapolis: The Bobbs-Merrill Co., 1966, anthologizes in addition some younger writers who would become prominent a few years later: Langston Hughes, Nathanael West, and Richard Wright. A look back from the perspective of the 1960s is to be found in a special issue of the magazine *The Carleton Miscellany*, Winter, 1965. Few of the writer-contributors are well known, but their recollections are often warm, intimate, and revealing. Recently published is *Jack Salzman with Barry Wallenstein, eds., *Years of Protest: A Collection of American Writings of* *the 1930's*, New York: Pegasus, 1967, with some 70 selections. The hot-tempered POLITICS of the period are coolly re-examined in a group of retrospective essays gathered in *Rita James Simon, ed., *As We Saw the Thirties: Essays on Social and Political Movements of the Decade*, Urbana: University of Illinois Press, 1967. The spectrum runs from racist right to the Socialists, Communists, and Trotskyites.

The best book on LABOR for the Thirties is *Irving Bernstein, *The Lean Years*, Baltimore: Penguin Books, 1966. He describes the workers' ups and downs from 1920 to 1933. It is a big book, but never dull.

A beautiful and agonizing picture-text documentary on TENANT FARMERS is *James Agee and Walker Evans, *Let Us Now Praise Famous Men*, New York: Ballantine Books, 1966. The writer and photographer, poets both, lived with the three families whose lives they picture with great honesty and dignity.

A compact illustrated history of the fate of BLACK AMERICA during the depression is found in *Milton Meltzer and August Meier, *Time of Trial, Time of Hope: The Negro in America, 1919–1941*, New York: Doubleday and Company (Zenith), 1966. A personal story of life in Harlem is told by a black social worker, Anna Arnold Hedgeman, in *The Trumpet Sounds*, New York: Holt, Rinehart and Winston, 1964. Malcolm X, a child at the time of the depression, recalls family life on welfare in the first chapters of *The Autobiography of Malcolm X*, New York: Grove Press, 1966. The photographer, writer, and film-maker, Gordon Parks, has also recorded the depression years in his powerful autobiography, *A Choice of Weapons*, New York: Berkley, 1967.

Periodicals

The richest sources of firsthand material are newspapers and magazines, and certain magazines far more so than most newspapers. Though both bring the period to life—with advertisements, the latest movies, and other events of the day—the press seems to have assumed that lack of confidence was partly responsible for the depression and tended to ignore or play down depression news, at least in the early period. The majority of newspaper publishers were Republican as well, and so usually handled the news in a way that would do least damage to their party and their president. Reporters, however, had no such stake in things as they were; and some, shaken by what they saw, found they had great freedom to write the facts— and their own responses—in such liberal magazines as the *Nation* and *New Republic. Harper's Magazine,* the *Atlantic Monthly, The American Mercury,* and *The Survey* (the last two now defunct) also carried first-rate reporting. I have drawn heavily on the *Nation* and *New Republic* especially, and recommend their reporting by such writers as Edmund Wilson, John Dos Passos, Malcolm Cowley, Marquis W. Childs, Matthew Josephson, Mauritz Hallgren, and Mary Heaton Vorse.

Most of these magazines can be found in bound volumes or on microfilm in public and university libraries, and possibly high school libraries ought to attempt to secure a file on one or another of them.

Photography

With the coming of the New Deal, photographers such as Gordon Parks, John Vachon, Dorothea Lange, Carl Mydans, Ben Shahn, and others photographed America for the Farm Security Administration. Their extraordinary artistic record— over 65,000 prints—is housed in the Library of Congress in Washington. High school students may use the library only by special written permission, but some of the photographs have been published. To list a few books: *Walker Evans, *American Photographs,* New York: The Museum of Modern Art,

1962; *Dorothea Lange and Paul Schuster Taylor, *An American Exodus*, New York: The Museum of Modern Art, 1962; and (out of print) Richard Wright with Edwin Rosskam, photographer, *12 Million Black Voices*, New York: The Viking Press, 1941.

Songs

The depression was rich in music if little else. Perhaps the greatest of the depression minstrels was Woody Guthrie, and a good collection is *California to the New York Island*, New York: Oak Publications, 1960. Songs of labor and unions are found in *Edith Fowke and Joe Glazer, eds., *Songs of Work and Freedom*, New York: Doubleday and Company (Dolphin), 1961. There is also *Waldemar Hill, ed., *People's songbook*, New York: Oak Publications, 1961; and many popular ballads are gathered in *H. Wood, ed., *New Lost Ramblers songbook*, New York: Oak Publications, 1964. In *The Ballad of America: The History of the United States in Song and Story*, New York: Bantam Books (Pathfinder), 1966, ed. John Anthony Scott devotes a chapter to songs of the depression years.

As for records, there are, among others, the New Lost City Ramblers' *Songs of the Depression*, Folkways FH 5264; and *Songs of the Depression and the New Deal*, Heirloom Records, Ed. 1, a recording made by high school students.

ACKNOWLEDGMENTS

Grateful acknowledgment is made for permission to reprint from the following:

A *Choice of Weapons* by Gordon Parks, copyright © 1965, 1966 by Gordon Parks, reprinted by permission of Harper & Row Publishers, Inc.

"Brother, Can You Spare a Dime?" copyright 1932 by Harms, Inc., used by permission.

California to the New York Island by Woody Guthrie, copyright © 1958 and 1960, reprinted by permission of The Guthrie Children's Trust Fund.

Child Workers in America by Katharine DuPre Lumpkin and Dorothy Wolff Douglas, copyright 1937, reprinted by permission of International Publishers Co., Inc. (47–48, 136–138).

Esquire, from the June 1960 issue, copyright © 1960 by John Steinbeck, reprinted by permission of McIntosh and Otis, Inc. (75–76).

Fortune, reprinted from the February 1933 issue by special permission, copyright © 1933 Time, Inc.

Infidel in the Temple by Matthew Josephson, copyright 1967, reprinted by permission of Alfred A. Knopf, Inc. (83–84, 87–88).

New Republic, August 17, 1932, reprinted by permission of Malcolm Cowley; and May 13, 1933, © 1933, 1961 by Emily Hahn, reprinted by permission of Brandt & Brandt.

"Pastures of Plenty," words and music by Woody Guthrie, TRO © copyright 1960 and 1963, Ludlow Music, Inc., New York, N.Y. Used by permission.

Proletarian Literature in the U.S., ed. by Granville Hicks *et al.*, copyright 1935 by International Publishers Co., Inc. (141–142).

Sanity Is Where You Find It: An Affectionate History of the United States in the 20's and 30's by America's Best-Loved Comedian by Will Rogers, copyright 1955, reprinted by permission of Houghton Mifflin Co.

Seeds of Revolt by Mauritz Hallgren, copyright 1933, reprinted by permission of Curtis Brown, Ltd.

"Soup Song," reprinted by permission of Maurice Sugar.

The American Earthquake by Edmund Wilson, copyright 1958, reprinted by permission of the author (81, 83, 114–116).

The Carleton Miscellany, copyright 1965 by Carleton College, reprinted by permission of *The Carleton Miscellany* (71–75).

The Theme Is Freedom by John Dos Passos, copyright 1938 and 1956, published by Dodd, Mead & Co. (85–87, 150–152).

These Are Our Lives by the Federal Writers' Project, Works Progress Administration; copyright © 1939, reprinted by permission of the University of North Carolina Press (42–43).

The Trumpet Sounds by Anna Arnold Hedgeman, copyright © 1964 by Anna Arnold Hedgeman, reprinted by permission of Holt, Rinehart and Winston, Inc.

Grateful acknowledgment is made for the use of illustrations:

American National Red Cross, 122; Emil J. Arnold, 39; Brown Brothers, 8, 164; Chicago Historical Society, 66, 149; Condé Nast Publications, Inc., reprinted from *Vanity Fair*, copyright 1932 (renewed 1960), 31, 69; Culver Pictures, Inc., 11, 89, 94; Library of Congress, Farm Security Administration, 44, 61, 117, 131, 138, 143; Museum of Modern Art, 79, 82; Museum of the City of New York, 56; National Archives, Works Projects Commission, 26; National Archives, U.S. Signal Corps, 154; New York *Daily News*, 156; New York Public Library, 18, 96, 113; State Historical Society of Wisconsin, © New York *Herald Tribune*, Inc., 21; United Press International, 167.

The jacket is a detail from "Reading from Left to Right" by Raphael Soyer, collection of Emil J. Arnold, courtesy of the Forum Gallery, New York City. The frontispiece is among the photographs from the Farm Security Administration, a collection that usually dates two to five years after the period of this book.

INDEX

Wiggin, Albert, 93, 95

Wilson, Edmund, 58–59, 81, 83, 114–116, 150

Wilson, Woodrow, 6, 161

Woods, Arthur, 92

World War I, 6, 13, 17, 20, 22, 57, 88, 93, 107, 121, 150, 153, 155, 158

Brother, Can You Spare a Dime? was originally published in the Living History Library, a series of books which provide a fresh, challenging, and human approach to the study of the American past. The overall theme of the series is the history of the United States as told by the people who shaped it and lived it. In each book, songs, documents, letters, and diaries are joined by a sustaining commentary to illuminate a given facet or topic in the history of the American people.

The general editor of the Living History Library is John Anthony Scott. He has taught at every level from junior high school to graduate school—at Fieldston School, Amherst College, Columbia University, and Rutgers University School of Law. Mr. Scott is the author of several books, including *Settlers on the Eastern Shore* and *Trumpet of a Prophecy: Revolutionary America*; editor of *Living Documents in American History*; and co-editor of *The Diary of the American Revolution*.